SEARCH FOR THE LOST PLANTATIONS
OF FLAGLER COUNTY, FLORIDA

ALSO BY WILLIAM RYAN

The Search For Old King's Road

I Am Grey Eyes

Bulow Gold

Door To Time In Florida

Osceola - His Capture And Seminole Legends

SEARCH FOR THE LOST PLANTATIONS
OF FLAGLER COUNTY, FLORIDA

WILLIAM P. RYAN

SEARCH FOR THE LOST PLANTATIONS
OF FLAGLER COUNTY, FLORIDA

Copyright © 2015 William P. Ryan

All rights reserved. No part of this publication may be reproduced, stored in a retrieval system or transmitted by any means including electronic, mechanical photocopying, recording, or otherwise, except brief extracts for the purpose of review, without the permission of the copyright owner.

Printed in the United States of America
First Printing 2015

ISBN-13: 978-1517461157
ISBN-10: 1517461154

www.oldkingsroad.com

Table of Contents

Preface 9
1 - So Begins My Search 1
2 - The Dead Mules 4
3 - Grants From 1766 to 1821 9
4 - The Land Grant Documents 14
5 - The Dupont Story 17
6 - Abraham Dupont Begins a New Legacy 25
7 - A Visit to the Dupont Memory 28
8 - Luke Is Baptized 39
9 - Joseph Marion Hernandez – 1792 to 1857 41
10 - Hernandez and a Colonial Era Sea Port 48
11 - Hernandez - MalaCompra Plantation 54
12 - Bella Vista Plantation Now A State Park 64
St. Joseph's Plantation – Lost and Forgotten 69
13 - We Live In a Different World 76
14 - The Florida Past 78
15 - Many Flags and Many People 80
16 - Slaves Escape into Florida 83
17 - What Might Have Been? 89
18 - Graham's Swamp – John Graham 94
19 - Listing of Spanish Grants in Flagler County 100
20 - The Pellicer Plantation 109
21 - Jesse Fish Deserves a Full Book 112
22 - In Reward for Services to the King 115
23 - The Spanish Surveyor 123
24 - We Must Have a Good Road 126
25 - A Plantation for Trees – Hewitt's Mill 131
26 - Fort Fulton February 21, 1840 136
Shipbuilder John Russell 139
27 - July 10, 1831 Spanish Flag is Removed 142
28 - The Bulow Family of Charleston 145
29. - The Legend of an Indian Princess 148
30 - The Building of a Plantation 150
31 - Housing for the Plantation Workers 154
32 - The Bulow Plantation House 158
33 - Considering Slavery 160

34 - Sugar Production at Bulow Plantation Ruins 167
35 - A Dye Stuff as Valuable as Gold 175
36 - Bulow Rice Fields? 178
37 - John James Audubon Visits Bulow in 1831 179
38 - The Distant Thunder of Evil..................................... 183
39 - Technology, Planning and Dreams Vanish 186
40 - The Causes of War 189
41 - The 'Mosquito Roarers'..191
42 - The Battle of Dunlawton 195
43 - Were They 'Taken' or Did They Join? 200
44 - The Slave Camp at Anastasia Island 204
45 - An Indian Camp on Haw Creek.............................. 209
46 - May 7, 1836: Death of John Joachim Bulow............ 213
47 - Florida's Atlantic Side Plantations 219
48 - The Early Plantations Are Gone...............................226
49 - Memories of the Past... 228
50 - I Became a Teller of Stories.....................................229
About the Author 231
Endnotes..233

Preface

It was the regular Wednesday meeting of the 'Bunnell Boy's Club' within the small green block building, almost hidden behind the old Holden House Museum in the small village of Bunnell, Florida.

The historical men and women (ladies were welcomed too) loved to talk history, of times past, in their somewhat rambling, non-directed conversations. One or two would glance at the door hoping for a fresh visitor. Few would arrive in the inclement Florida winds of January.

Relatives appeared on every wall in faded pictures showing the rich 1918 to 1940's era when this small Florida town prospered, and the trains still stopped here. This author was a Yankee. I arrived from Chicago, but then so did many of the 'outsiders' in the growing city of Palm Coast that had overcome this small village. I was not much interested in long dead uncles and cousins. I wanted to talk about some really old history. The conversations would not go in that direction.

"Did you know we had over 27 land grants and maybe plantations from the British and second Spanish colonial periods right here in what would become Flagler County?"

I asked this hoping someone would take up the topic.

"Look, it's right here in this report," I tried again while holding a copy of the ***Palm Coast Cultural Resource Assessment*** paper written by Professor James J. Miller in July of 1978.

"Hold that thought, I'll be right back," said Sisco Deen, the main museum 'collector" who rose, went to the back map store room. He unrolled a large map on the table. It showed listings of "land grants," labeled and designated by a State Surveyor in the 1930's.

"Here they are. If they were 'plantations' then you may wish to look for them. Most are forgotten," he said.

Now I had a map.

1 - So Begins My Search

The old map showed the location of some large Flagler land grants. Could there really have been over 27 "plantations" right here? Here would be huge now forgotten enterprises going back over 230 years!

But where are the Dupont works on this map? I could not find them. I took the large map to the County Clerk's office. Fortunately, they were testing out a new digital scanner so this map could now be viewed in detail on any computer. There was another tool available too. The Spanish land grants were also offered in digital form on the *Florida Memories* website.

Flagler County Florida is between St. Augustine and tourist oriented Daytona Beach on Florida's Atlantic coast. Until the great economic crash they called a "Recession" it was listed as one of the fastest growing areas in Florida, full of growing gated developments, shopping malls and anxious real estate agents that featured the Florida dream. The new city of Palm Coast had originated from a great Florida developer called ITT. So much history has been forgotten here with the great waves of developers seeking to mine the Florida estate gold. I knew there was land speculation here even going back before the American Revolution when England held Florida. Could this old map reveal plantations now forgotten?

There were few markers to the past here. If you were fortunate to find the touring signs and were directed past the stores and shops to a short piece of "The Old King's Road" which was built by the British, you might find a narrow path to what is called "***The Bulow Plantation Ruins Historic State Park***." It's not easy to locate.

These haunting ruins, located deep in a Florida wilderness, are open only Thursday through Monday. There are other ruins nearby, but what remains at Bulow has power. You can feel the flow of history or hear the forever silence of this destroyed dream when you stand near the smoke blackened ruin of the sugar mill.

What these ruins can tell you! They hint of the immense enterprises that once existed on Florida's Atlantic Coast. They began long ago when the British first held this Florida Colony, before the American Revolution. Consider the second period of ownership by Spain when the Spanish were anxious to develop their Florida lands. Or when Bulow arrived in 1821 to join the new land rush of American ownership and the later disastrous Indian war.

The old map was my guide. I noted its names, and read the Spanish land grant documents I found writings concerning this long lost era. Some of the larger plantations were well documented by historian Alice Strickland and others, but what happened to new names appearing on this old map? I must explain what I mean by 'plantation'. Spain under the second Spanish period had definite rules: farm for at least 10 years, raise structures, have a family and workers eg. Slaves, produce crops, have it surveyed and many other rules to obtain title of a grant. My rule is that they were here, had a real operation on their land and were much more than "a one horse farm."

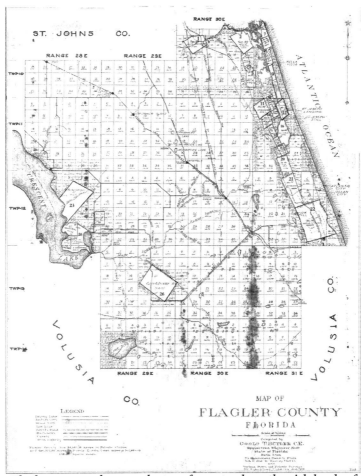

The large map shows a cluster of grants along the rich lands of Graham's Swamp. Numbers used were those identified in the Palm Coast Cultural Resources report, plus additional ones I added on grants given in Western Flagler County. I will repeat enlarged sections of this map to make it easier to locate areas. Many grants were sold and continued as plantations right up to the War Between the States period, and for some I did not find their story. Each area must have its own tale of hard work and often disaster

2 - The Dead Mules

Before I could study the map of Flagler plantations I was invited to visit a real one. Our Flagler County Historical Society met at a meeting at the Hewitt J. Dupont plantation site still occupied by the Dupont family. [1] Hewett Dupont then told this story that carried us into the past.

Hewitt Dupont addresses the Flagler County Historical Society under the old live oak trees of a Dupont plantation. Much of the old Dupont plantation here still exists. (Photo Flagler County Historical Society)

    For many years he said there was some animosity between the extensive Dupont and the Hernandez families. The Dupont held that Hernandez had taken their lands. There was also a family story of some wandering mules belonging to the Hernandez plantation that were shot by a Dupont slave.
    Like so many good stories in old Flagler County this one has many twists.
    "In the 1850's Joseph Hernandez had some mules. They would sometimes wander onto Dupont land, eat crops and cause a mess. One morning Adam, who was a slave for the Hernandez family, was walking on the King's Road between

the two plantations and found a Hernandez mule, shot dead beside the road. He later discovered two others badly wounded and would die.

Adam followed the blood trail to the Dupont plantation.

Luke who was a slave of Abraham Dupont was questioned and admitted he shot the mules at the instruction of Mr. Dupont. He later testified that if more mules came, he was ordered to shoot them too. Luke was then charged with "malicious destruction of property" which was the Florida penal code of 1832. There had been a prior penal code of 1828 that was not used and was much stronger. The real question was if Luke could exhibit free will when he was ordered to kill the mules by his master. If not, should the master be charged? Further Luke was carrying a firearm which now was absolutely against the rigorous slave laws passed around 1828 after the United States took over Florida from Spain in 1821. The more liberal Spanish codes relative to peoples of African origin were long vanished.

The Dupont's engaged a powerful lawyer, Mr. McQueen McIntosh, a decedent of a fine southern family. As a state attorney general he had been involved in a prosecution of a former Georgia governor for illegal importation of slaves. He was well acquainted with the laws regarding slaves. Another figure on the case for the Dupont's was James Pellicer assisting Mr. McIntosh.

A circuit court in St. Johns had found Dupont's slave Luke guilty of malicious mischief. He was sentenced to three months in jail and legal expenses to be paid by Dupont. With a barrage of legal documents McIntosh appealed saying the St. John's court had made technical errors. He argued that charges were made under the wrong slave law. It appears that Luke was not jailed awaiting the results of the appeal.

The case then ended up at the 1853 Florida Supreme Court.

This Mule incident was a hot potato.

If under the law Luke had no will of his own, other than that of his master, then should not his master be charged with the crime, and Luke held blameless?

The court could not decide which laws to apply.

The rights of slaves or the rights of their master were not subjects a Florida court wished to address.

So they avoided the entire matter and did not rule at all. The case was dismissed on a technicality of the initial charge being made under the wrong law. The United States was then a slave country and the position of a person of African heritage had no place in the current legal system... Certainly a slave could not be admitted as a participant to a court trial where a white man might be at risk!

Also the idea of a slave having a weapon to carry out his master's orders would be a subject no Florida planter wished to discuss.

These appeals and legal maneuvering were costing money and required sizeable deposits to the state. Rather than having a judgment by the court the conviction was finally set aside on a technical point of law. It is not known whether the slave Luke really did any time in jail.

The likely outcome of the 'Dead Mules' was very expensive lawyers for the Dupont family after they paid all legal bills to Mr. McQueen McIntosh. [2]

Now I want to move back a bit in time and give you some background.

Is history really linear? I don't think it always exists in dates and times, marching neatly in rows on a page.

I warn you now I will wander about in this story. I find that events often connect both forward and can go in reverse much like the errant Hernandez mules.

Grants of land brought men of daring

Spain held Florida for almost 200 years. Except for a series of Catholic missions to convert the natives, there was not a lot of land development during this time.

When England took over Florida, their King offered grants of land that were intended to bring in new settlers. Some of these Colonial land grant enterprises began in what today is known as Flagler County, Florida. (It once was called Mosquito County when it was part of Volusia!) An extensive area of rich soil here was to be known as Graham's Swamp. Here would cluster Colonial era plantations. The King's Road, built by the British about 1774, carried slaves, soldiers, raw sugar, cotton, wagons, stagecoaches and the many things needed for this new economy. Then came the second Spanish period when Spain returned after the American Revolution. Time would end for all of our planters when the Second Seminole War began on Christmas Eve of 1835 following the takeover of Florida by the United States in 1821.

Plantations of these times burned into crumbled rubble. Slaves labored and lived here their lives unrecorded, their graves unmarked. We know very little about them. Some historians have written that largest slave revolt that ever occurred in the U.S. happened here when many of the plantation slaves fled to join with the Indian warriors. [3] It is a story that was hidden in the then slave dependent south. This tale made few history books of the time. We were a nation that still supported a slave economy. News of any revolt would be suppressed.

The local Indians, now called Seminoles, raised cattle here and often traded profitably with the plantations. Grants of land which began under the King of England were greatly expanded when Spain supported the American Revolution and then was rewarded with a second ownership of Florida in 1783. To expand the riches of Florida people were needed here, brave entrepreneurs and a slave labor force. Huge grants of free land would be the magnet.

In 1786, the Spanish Court of Madrid gave permission for the few British subjects still in Florida to keep their land titles after swearing allegiance. A few were successful with recorded claims in what would become Flagler County. In 1790, King Charles IV of Spain had approved hundreds of new land grants to attract settlers. These numbers increased dramatically when the United States desired Florida and the Spanish perhaps suspected they might have to depart forever when Florida became a U.S. Territory. In 1821 a land hungry United States took control of Florida, and many new settlers arrived to purchase or seize these early Spanish land grants.

Thus free land had brought forth the men of vision, of courage, and hope who were willing to invest their lives in the promise of Florida under British and then Spanish rule. They would now have to prove their ownership to the new Americans. Often only the names on these odd documents are all that remain to tell us of the existence of these grantees, to trace their dreams.

Today only few pieces of moss overgrown, cut coquina rock might rest in forgotten woodland to mark where the plantation houses or slave quarters of great enterprise once existed. These artifacts were photographed during a visit to "Hernandez Landing" area prior to its development as a nature park. Many relicts vanish or are covered by development.

3 - Grants From 1766 to 1821

More than 27 known land grants in Flagler County [4]

Spain in St. Augustine 1565 – 1763
British in Florida 1763 – 1783 (British grants)
Spain returns to Florida 1783 – 1821 (Spanish grants)
Florida US Territory 1821 – 1845
Florida as a state - 1845
Florida withdraws from Union January 10 1861
State of Florida returns 1868

Florida land grants were issued during the British Period and many more during the second Spanish occupation. Only a few of the British were able to hold their lands when Spain took over Florida following the American Revolution. The website *Florida Memories* [5] lists over 932 land grants made by Spain. [6] Many of the Spanish grant documents were more artistic than accurate surveys.

The King's Road built by the British in 1774 was often the only reference for location. These early grants by the British King and the King of Spain had to be proven when the U.S. took over Florida. This provided profitable employment for lawyers during the later years when U.S. legislation required proofs of ownership in Florida. Recorded names now fade into our past. The plantations are long vanished. Only these old documents remain to record the human enterprise, the life of slaves and the dreams of new settlers; those that built the plantations of Florida and began to settle what would become Flagler County.

The legend of family disputes still remains after so many years. Many grants were sold, or later mortgaged and would pass several owners. However, Flagler still has several "old families" such as the Dupont, [7] Pellicer, and Russell who trace their ancestry back to the original British or Spanish grants, often some 200 years or more.

"You are not truly gone until they forget your name"- Grey Eyes

The Adams-Onis Treaty of 1819 gave Florida to the United States but said that land grants given by the Spanish would be honored by the Americans provided the grantees had met all of the Spanish grant conditions. Coppinger had resisted turning documents over when his soldiers marched out of the fort in July of 1821. There was fear they would vanish when the Americans got them. Proof of true ownership might become impossible against what he believed about the greedy Americans wanting new lands in Florida.

When the United States took over its new territory of Florida from Spain in July of 1821 affairs went well although there was mistrust between the local Spanish officials and the new ones from the US about the Spanish documents. The remaining Spanish officer Col. Jose Coppinger y Gamarra had long struggled to retain control of them without support from the weak, almost nonexistent Spanish government in St. Augustine. Now he was behind locked doors in the decrepit Government House in St. Augustine guarding large stacks of papers that reflected the many land grants given by the King of Spain to settlers in Florida.

On October 2, 1821, a party of American soldiers with the new Governor Worthington broke the locks of Government House and took away cartons of his important documents. Yes, it was agreed in the Treaty of cession in 1819 that Spanish authorities would give these to the Americans, but Coppinger had feared they would then vanish. [8]

There were multitudes of these grants, many are known, and some are forgotten. The Spanish recorded the great and small plantation enterprises of early Florida.

With few exceptions, nothing remains of these works in the wilds of Florida except those referenced in surviving Spanish papers and those that made successful claims when the Americans took over Florida. Their travels make an interesting story as recorded in the *Florida Memory* electronic archives. Perhaps some did vanish as feared by Mr. Coppinger but that became a question for the lawyers

After the American authorities seized the Spanish documents, they held them at the Old Customs House and a commission was appointed to examine them and rule on the lands that had become US property by the treaty with Spain. Various officials were "keepers" of the archives. In August of 1823, the commission met and had set a deadline of November 1827 for all applications submitted from those wishing to establish the older British grants or the more recent Spanish grants. There was confusion and claims of fraud as the multitude of grantees and their heirs appeared to submit their documents to the commission.

There were rejections. For example, Francisca de Aguilar (Donna) had applied for 30,000 acres of "vacant land" along Haw Creek, middle branch. The commission rejection said it was "a forgery" or a "fraud" citing claims for defense against Indian attacks that the commission said did not happen. However, George Atkinson was awarded his 3,000 acres in middle Haw Creek around the same area.

It was not easy to hold onto a land grant. Spain had complicated rules to obtain land title. You had to farm for at least 10 years, have the land surveyed, erect buildings, have a labor force or slaves, grow a crop or otherwise clear and improve the place, and then meet the inspection of the Spanish authority. It was a complicated, lengthy procedure. It took many Spanish documents to obtain final title to your land. It appeared to me that these rules did not apply to everyone, depending on your status in the Spanish bureaucracy.

This might not always apply to powerful personages such as Hernandez or Don George Clarke, Captain of the Northern

Spanish District of East Florida and Surveyor General of the Provence. Hernandez or Clarke heirs performed many services for the Spanish government; their heirs were awarded many grants. While political pressures were intense, the Commission set up by the United States was faced with the some 900 Spanish Grants, a formidable task to decide on who owns which properties. Each applicant had to produce any documents, maps and sworn testimony and to prove their ownership of the land.

Can these large grants be known as "Plantations?" Many locations did have slaves, purchased machinery and steam engines, raised crops and did prove their right of occupation with the complex rules of the Spanish government. Then, when the Americans took charge, the proof was required again. Copy machines did not exist. Notarized copies and translations of Spanish documents made thick files and revenue for lawyers. Many land owners had continued to grow crops, build their houses, and utilize slaves, and continued their venture in Florida when the Spanish departed. Detailed reports are few but by this author's definition, many were **Plantations**.

The commission did rule that unless the Spanish had recognized the grants from the King of England in Florida, those claims would not be considered. The bulk of the English had departed when Spain took over following the American Revolution. Those that remained had to provide proof and a few accomplished this in what would become Flagler County.

Transfers of land made near the end of the Spanish rule, and some grants made by Spanish Governor Coppinger were looked at with suspicion by the commission. Along the Graham's swamp area, there were records of applications by George Webber, James Toote, and John Carter listed as "unconfirmed." The applications of the heirs of Valentine Fitzpatrick and McDowell and Black were shown as being confirmed. Sometimes a minor flaw in a submission kept a claim from being allowed. Having the artistic Spanish document did not always secure title. In 1811 shipwright John

Russell had swapped a fine ship for a land grant that would later be sold to Charles Wilhelm Bulow to launch his plantation in 1821 when the US took over Florida.

Some titles were established by marriage, as under Spanish law a male heir was required. In 1815 Joseph Hernandez married Ana Maria Hill, the widow of Samuel Williams, and acquired extensive property rights. He obtained many grant certificates from Spanish Governor Coppinger in 1817. These were verified for a huge total of 20,000 acres by the US land Commission in 1832. So in addition to the lands obtained by his marriage to Widow Hill and other grants he purchased from others, Hernandez owned a vast amount of Florida land. Some of his holdings were later heavily mortgaged. His St. Joseph Plantation was called "the most valuable plantation accessible by sail in Florida." [9] Jesse Fish also appears on the list of grants. He had acted as an agent for the desperate English planters when Spain took over Florida. Some grants were obtained by Gabriel W. Perpall who was named to be Mayor of St. Augustine when the Americans took over. (The new Governor Andrew Jackson forced reorganization that later removed Mr. Perpall.) In theory a grantee also had to prove he was using or improving the property such as erecting buildings or planting and harvesting crops.

Land might be granted for 'brave service' to the Spanish when the 'Patriots" were invading Florida in 1812. A large area appears to be designated in Western Flagler following Dunn's Lake (Crescent Lake). In September 1817 a similar grant for military service to Spain was given to Marten Hernandez who was Gen. Hernandez' father and a Minorcan hero. Many of these documents now appear on the ***Florida Memories*** internet site under Florida Spanish Land Grants. Even to lawyers at the time, ownership of these lands in Florida was confusing and subject to legal conflict. After the Americans took over in 1821 there was a great land rush into Florida as new enterprises began.

4 - The Land Grant Documents

In April 1823 President John Quincy Adams wrote to John Rodman, who was then Collector of Customs in St. Augustine to have William Reynolds and Antonio Alvarez examine the cases of Spanish documents which were in Mr. Rodman's custody. He wished any documents related to property in Florida retained and the balance given to Mr. Hernandez who was planning a trip to Havana Cuba and had offered to transport any Spanish documents which "did not relate to the Sovereignty, which Spain had over the Territory." [10] However, later letters indicate the records did not travel with Mr. Hernandez... The Spanish had departed two years prior and the Americans needed proof of their new land ownerships. The boxes of Spanish records were a real prize. It appeared that John Rodman, well known to Mr. Hernandez had possession.

(Copy of ltr Sisco Deen collection)
THE SECRETARY OF STATE TO JOHN RODMAN Department of State WASHINGTON 5 April 1823 JOHN RODMAN Esquire Collector of the Customs St Augustine

SIR Conformably to your Suggestion in your Letter of the 3d of December last, Mr. Reynold and Mr. Alvarez are authorized by the Letter, herewith enclosed, and which you will please deliver to them, to examine the eight Boxes of Documents and Archives, mentioned by you; to select from them, those which relate to the property and Sovereignty of East & West Florida, to be retained, and to cause the remainder to be repacked, to be returned to the Spanish Commanding Office at the Havana. Mr Hernandez before leaving this place, intimated his intention of visiting the Havana soon after his return home, and I hope the examination and selection may be completed, in time to forward by him the Documents to be returned. I am with much Respect,

Sir, your very humble and obedient Servant
[Enclosure]
The Secretary of State to William Reynolds and Antonio Alvarez
Department of State WASHINGTON 5 Apr 1823

REYNOLDS AND ANTONIO ALVAREZ Esq. St. Augustine. Florida.

SIRS You are hereby authorized to examine the contents of eight Boxes of Archives, which were taken by direction of Mr Worthington, while acting as Governor of East Florida, from the House of the late Spanish Governor Coppinger, and which are now under the charge of John Rodman Esquire, Collector of the Port of St Augustine; "to select from them for preservation among the Archives of the Territory," all Archives and Documents which relates directly to the property and Sovereignty, of the Provinces of East & West Florida, to take an Inventory of the same, and also of all other Documents, and papers, found among them; and carefully to cause to be packed up all those of the latter description, to be returned to the Governor or Captain General of the Island of Cuba, or to his order. Mr Reynolds as keeper of the Archives appointed by Governor Duval, will then take in charge the Documents to be retained, together with the inventory of those to be restored to the officer of the Spanish Government - The Documents themselves to be returned may be delivered to **Mr Hernandez** (*bf by author*) for that purpose, taking his receipt and promise to have them so delivered, unless before this examination and Selection shall be completed, he shall embarked for the Havana. In which· case they may be retained by Mr Reynolds, until he shall receive further directions concerning them from this Department. For this service you will each receive five dollars per day; and such reasonable charges, as may be occasioned by the taking of the Inventory, and the packing for transportation the Documents to be returned. I am with much Respect, Gentlemen, your very humble and obedient Servant

JOHN QUINCY ADAMS
Transcribed for the Flagler County Historical Society by Sisco Deen, November 1, 2014

In 1942, The US Government under the Works Progress Administration (WPA) began a project to record and consolidate the Spanish land grant records. These old Spanish documents were studied by Professor E. V. Gage of Florida State College and published in *Spanish Land Grants in Florida*. The on-line listing of these under *Florida Memory/Spanish grants* is extensive, and while perhaps not complete, it opened the door for me to do many hours of study, and much ink while printing off the more interesting ones.

Many now appear on the Florida Memories website which lists collections by approved and rejected grants along with their Spanish wording and English translation. But not all are available, especially those of the early Duponts.

5 - The Dupont Story

While searching my old map, I found many "plantations" or land grants listed but none with the Dupont name. When I opened the Florida Memories web site to look up their collection of old Spanish land grants, I found many such under the Hernandez name but the Dupont papers that appeared were those from the relatives of Josiah Dupont seeking to restore their ownership to lands. These were refused by the US grant commission. Where were the Dupont original documents since he was one of the earliest ones to arrive here? The Spanish grants for Josiah did not appear in the extensive collection of the on-line history collection of Spanish grants. I saw a pattern as I dug deeper with hints here and there and after a very hot July visit to the St. Augustine Historical Library.

At times when you try to understand events from so long ago, it is like seeing distant summer heat lightning; you can see a weak red flash but not the rumble of the bolt. As I read documents held at the St. Augustine library, I found many were written by John C. Hall, who seemed to be the "Boswell" [11] of the extensive Dupont and Peter Buyck clans. Then Synergism arose again (read *Door to Time in Florida*.) I had many strange happenings while I did history research. A letter arrived at the Flagler Beach Museum from Mr. Hall enclosing his book on the Peter Buyck [12] family, who were related to the Dupont clan by marriage. Museum director Terry Pruden permitted me to read it, with the fascinating chapters on the Dupont family. The letter was written on an old typewriter, I recognized the type face from my 1950 Navy days.

But allow me to get back to my story.

After the British departed in 1783 the Spanish had inherited a very empty Florida. By the 1790's they were encouraging active settlement. Large British plantations such as that of John Moultrie, once lieutenant governor of British Florida, were abandoned. New settlers were now looking at the rich areas of hammock and black loam now called Graham's Swamp after former British settler John Graham. Old maps still showed some of the former English enterprises such as a "lime kiln" or orange grove location said to be about 3 miles South of Penjon inlet. Here once existed some of the 1,000 acres British grant to Mr. Moultrie.

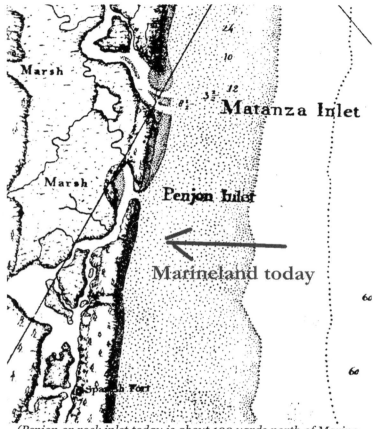

(Penjon or rock inlet today is about 100 yards north of Marineland, its opening presently closed until the ocean decides otherwise again. The lime kiln probably used oyster shells as its main source was likely nearby) [13]

In 1791 Josiah Dupont (b-1742 d-1802) arrived here from South Carolina. According to author Alice Strickland, he was given verbal permission to settle lands near the Matanzas River, south of St. Augustine, and had farmed for one year before he received a Spanish grant. Historian Sisco Deen has written that Josiah also had served as a surveyor for the Spanish government. He was to clear and develop his lands for some 10 years. Josiah Dupont and his family remained here until the Indian attacks of 1802. He would die at age 61 shortly after returning to South Carolina. There were indications that the lands he maintained were large, but records seem fuzzy. Josiah and his wife Anna [14] had the following children:

Abraham 1768
Anna or Ann 1770
Gideon 1772
Juana Isabel 1775
Maria Magdalena 1777
Isabelle 1779
Rebecca 1789

It appears that not all of Josiah's lands were surveyed by the Spanish. In 1792 he had applied for official grants equal to half the lands due him on the basis of head rights for himself, his wife, 7 children and 27 slaves. His request called for lands in two prime places:

1. South by 10 miles from "the little port of Matanzas at the head of the last salt water creek," also known as the East Prong of the Matanzas River.

2. On "Grahams Creek" in Grahams Swamp for a total of 1,850 acres. [15]

The Josiah Dupont family settled in what later would become the MalaCompra plantation of Joseph M. Hernandez. Dupont historian John Hall observed that the ruins of MalaCompra in the Flagler Bing's landing park were actually on top of a much older plantation structure built by Josiah Dupont. The Park signage mentions Dupont but not his house.

In 1793 Augustine Buyck had moved to Florida. A neighbor to Josiah Dupont he was developing a plantation to the south "on the east prong of the Matanzas River." (12 Sec. 38 – 632 acres.)

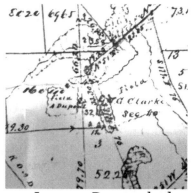

Some of his land was on 'Murritt's Old Field' which indicates someone may have been there before. Murritt's lies on Abraham Dupont's land, which was later occupied by Mr. and Mrs. Jack Dupont and is in SE ¼ section, 14 T10SR30E, south of the Princess Place preserve (Pellicer plantation)

In 1794 Dupont had a rice crop of about 50 barrels burned by an Indian attack. Thus rice was one of his important crops. Indian raids could be a serious problem as Spain had only a weak control over Florida; the soldiers in St. Augustine were often without pay. The Spanish were weak against raiders.

On August 9, 1800 a militia company commanded by General Georges (Jorge) Biassou, a former slave from Haiti, and now a general in the Spanish army, arrived to protect the Dupont property. He had arrived with 23 followers called 'Black Auxiliaries.' [16] Biassou was a true 'hot potato' for governor Quesada in St. Augustine. During the Haiti slave rebellion against the French Planters his men killed thousands of the Spanish French enemies. Thus Spain had made him a general. He wore uniforms shining with gold trim plus a Spanish gold medal. He arrived in St. Augustine with his followers and expected to be treated appropriate to his rank. There was no mention of it but perhaps as an important personage he might have attended a Dupont society wedding in St. Augustine.

Biassou died in July of 1801 so his Black Auxiliaries who were fierce warriors from Hispaniola may have departed leaving the Dupont lands undefended in 1802. His gold medal was melted down to pay the Biassou debts.

On 6 October 1800 Josiah's daughter Ann had been married to Augustine Buyck. [17] August Buyck was from a Flemish family who arrived in South Carolina from Flanders (now Belgium). The Dupont family was of Huguenot or Protestant heritage, while the Buyck family was Catholic. The new family moved south to a location where he was developing his new plantation to be called "Buycks Hammock/St. Anns Plantation."

This was puzzling as it was marked on my old map which shows it as a Hernandez property (12 – Sec. 38, 632 acres) with the modern Intracoastal canal running through its western side, and Hernandez's St. Joseph plantation marked to the west. I believe there was a possibility that Mr. Buyck had not obtained a Spanish survey and title but was working the land prior to obtaining a grant. No record of him again appeared in the Florida Memories website listing of Spanish grants. He was also drafted into the Spanish army which may have limited his development of the property.

Augustine and Ann were married in St. Augustine by father Miguel Crosby, listed in their lengthy marriage contract as a 'deacon' priest. Thus Crosby would be very familiar with this young family and the Dupont clan. I read their complex marriage contract. [18]

Author John Hall wrote that the Augustine/Buyck site is located on the east end of the Palm Coast Parkway toll bridge. Also in the same Hammock area is the Russell Hardware store, the family that would later sell land that would become the Bulow Plantation in 1821.

Josiah Dupont had obtained his Spanish lands near the headwaters of the Matanzas River from Governor Quesada in 1794. He lived there and cultivated his land until 1802, some 11 years, certainly raising crops, building structures and meeting the Spanish regulations. I do not know if he actually completed all of their complex requirements. Since he was also a Spanish surveyor and thus an official, let us assume he did. The Spanish documents of his occupancy seem to have vanished.

Indian raiders now would arrive to capture the valuable

Dupont slaves. They also killed and carried off a neighboring family named Bonelli. [19] Josiah's neighbor who was Joseph Bonelli Sr. who received several grants including one for 600 acres at Matanzas Bar.

In January 1802 while Mr. Bonelli was away on business, the Indians hit the Bonelli and Dupont farms. The "Miccosukee" Indians killed Bonelli's young son Thomas. His wife Maria Moll Bonelli and five younger children were taken to the Gulf area as captives. He later had to sell his grant to raise money for ransom.

The attacks may have originated with William Augustus Bowles, an Englishman who became an Indian leader in 1781 and opposed the Spanish. He had two Indian wives and adopted Indian dress and manner.

On January 5, 1802, he led a large force of Miccosukee Indians, runaway slaves, pirates, and Spanish rebels in a series of raids. The Indians who looted the Josiah Dupont property in 1802 came from this group. [20]

Dupont and his family escaped with their lives but lost everything. "`They had between thirty and forty working hands and a large stock of cattle here, at one time several hundred." [21] Josiah died one month later perhaps from the shock of losing everything to the raiders.

The Buyck family also departed Florida following the Indian attack returning to South Carolina. A relative called Gideon Dupont (1712-1789) (same name as Josiah's son) owned a plantation in Orangeburgh District, S.C. He would be Ann Buyck's grandfather, so she had relatives there.

The Dupont family had long believed that their lands were "taken" by Mr. Hernandez. Mr. Hernandez was in Washington some time prior to April 1823. He did appear in a letter from then Secretary of State John Quincy Adams relating plans for the distribution or disposition of the 8 boxes of Spanish documents that had been seized from former Spanish Governor Coppinger's residence. Hernandez was mentioned as a possibility for returning those documents not related to land ownership back to authorities in Cuba as he had planned such a trip. I might speculate he had some access to the documents. Members of the Dupont family held that Hernandez had irregular influence over the family's failure to obtain their lands back from the Spanish authorities.

Here I also speculate a bit. Certain lands of Josiah were re-granted to Father Michael (Miguel) Crosby, the Catholic priest in February 1804, two years after Josiah Dupont departed from St. Augustine. Some 11 years passed before the relatives of Dupont filed formal claims for their lands. Mr. Hernandez was now occupying them. It is a puzzlement to me how a Catholic priest in St. Augustine could own large amounts of former Dupont land.

In their claim documents the Duponts stated they left a manager and some "old Negroes" on the land but apparently they had vanished. Could Priest Crosby have some power with the Spanish establishment? Or was he what might be called 'a middle man' in a real estate deal? He certainly did know the Dupont family well.

Hernandez purchased some of the area land in 1815 from Crosby and called it MalaCompra. [22] He also purchased lands from a John Bautista Ferreyra and his son Francis. John Bautista was signed on as a witness with Priest Crosby at the Ann Dupont/Anthony Buyck wedding in St. Augustine so he too was knowledgeable of the Dupont lands.

The Dupont heirs later offered claims before the new US Commissioners on October 10, 1823. These were rejected. They disputed that the Dupont family had "abandoned" their lands. There would later be years of litigation by the Dupont and the Buyck families

> And your Memorialist further sheweth, that their Ancestor the said Josiah Dupont was in actual possession of said lands, from 1794 till 1802 when he was Obliged to abandon the same for a time on account of the depredations of the Indians, and dying about one month after leaving the same the same was not resumed till about two years one of the heirs attempted to return, but was prevented by persons who had taken possession with out the consent of the owners. That they are all citizen of the United States and resident of South Carolina
>
> John B. Strong
> St Augustine Oct 18th 1823 — Atty for Claimants

6 - Abraham Dupont Begins a New Legacy

An Abraham Dupont and his family moved into this area in 1825 calling his new property "Buena Veriro." [23] Abraham was the son of a Charles Dupont who was a revolutionary war soldier from Charleston. (He was not the same Abraham Dupont who was the son of Josiah Dupont. Josiah was this Abraham's uncle.) Josiah had named one of his sons Abraham and the other Gideon.

On August 25, 1828, he purchased land (7 – Sec. 38, township 10 south, range 31E) from Gabriel W. Perpall. It was some 700 acres bounded by the River Matanzas to the west, seashore to the east, and south by Joseph M. Hernandez's land. (8 – Sec. 39) It was here Abraham established his summer home in what today would be called "The Hammock" located off A1A south of Marineland. He lived there for 29 years. Abraham Dupont died in 1857. He was also said to have launched a town in 1828 on the west side of the Matanzas River south of Pellicer Creek, called "Matanzas" which in 1829 had a population of 50 and one Methodist Church. [24] In 1845 it listed the following as leading families: [25]

John Pellicer
John Sanders
William Wilkey
Jacob B. Sole
Abraham Dupont
Jacob Mickler
Francis Pellicer – he once managed Bulowville
James Pellicer – celebrated "mule" case

Matthew Long
Vahiel Brown

The Dupont family remained in an active role for the growth of what would someday become Flagler County, Florida. Abraham is buried in the Dupont cemetery, located west of the present A1A highway (Ocean shore Blvd.) in northern Flagler County, just south of the Marineland Park. Josiah Dupont had occupied extensive lands including what would become the MalaCompra Plantation of Hernandez. When his heirs later applied for their return, the original Spanish documents did not appear. The Abraham Dupont family consisted of 13 children with his first wife Jane Verdier Pepper, the ones I could find were:

Virgil Dupont – born 26 March 1813, SC or NC died 22 August 1885 and buried in Dupont Cemetery. He was the oldest son of Abraham. Lived on Matanzas plantation inherited from Abraham. His decedents have continuously lived on this land. Two sons William and Abraham served in Confederate army, Abraham died of wounds after the Battle of Seven Pines, and buried in Richmond Va. [26] William died in Volusia in 1862. Their names are on St. Augustine monument across the street from the Trinity Church where his father Abraham was one of its three founders.

Maria Olivia Dupont Hemming – born August 7, 1824. Married Charles W. Hemming. Received land north of St. Augustine in Abraham's will.

Cornelius Dupont – born 7 August 1824 died 1877. He lived on the St. John's River, called Dupont's Landing and returned there after serving in the Confederate army. In March of 1843, under the "Armed Occupation Act" which was intended to bring back settlers after the second Seminole War, he petitioned and obtained 160 acres of property in Section 14, Range 30E,T.S.10, which would lie near the old Josiah Dupont's "Murrets Field" lands. [27]

Benjamin Dupont – Born 25 December 1825 died 26 January 1911. Buried in Dupont Cemetery. Served in Confederate army. Inherited plantation on east side of Matanzas River from Abraham, the location known today as

The Hammock.
Elizabeth Veredier Dupont – Born 7 February 1823

7 - A Visit to the Dupont Memory

If the Dupont family held a complete reunion, they most likely would fill a football stadium. I am asked if they are related to the 'dynamite' Dupont to the north. Perhaps in the far past they are, but it is not my purpose to do a genealogical study here. There are many who can do this far better. The story of the Flagler County Dupont families is one of successful farming, plantations and hard work.

"We were the quiet ones, and did not get much publicity," said Hewitt Dupont who with his wife Allene Dupont launched me on an exploration.

We began on a hot July day guided by Hewitt Dupont. Here was the site of the old Dupont sugar mill. Time had left very little but you could still feel that something important had once been here. The busy farms were overgrown now but the crops and hard working men were not so far away as time goes. Is the generation of lives really that far away from us?

Quoting from the Palm Coast Cultural Evaluation Report: "Murrit's (sp) Oldfield corresponds to Abraham Dupont's field noted on the plat of 1850 of A.M. Randolph. The homestead is presently occupied by Mr. and Mrs Jack Dupont (*Hewitt Dupont's father and mother*). It is situated in the SE ¼ of Section 14, T10SR30E." This pleasant live oak hammock surrounded by second growth vegetation and pine plantations was probably occupied after the Second Seminole War. In 1844 the house was noted as a mail stop along the

King's Road. The remains of the original house, now mostly scattered coquina, are located just east of the Dupont's garden and shed. Nineteenth century artifacts, mostly black glass and pottery, can be found occasionally in the yard."

Some 1500 feet west of the house is a pine island within swampy land where slave quarters once stood. According to Mr. Dupont if this area is driven east to west, ridges remaining from the rice fields may be recognized as distinct bumps. East of this area, now partly in planted pines, is tidal marsh and swamp forming the head of Styles Creek, and then another dry landform upon which are found the remains of the Dupont mill." [28]

Covered by dirt and leaf is the sugar line of the Dupont Mill. The fire bricks remain.

There are coquina and brick pieces scattered about. The bricks are the red squared type that I noted were identical to those I saw in the sugar line of the Bulow Plantation. What appeared to be the actual sugar line of heated kettles lay under leaf and soil but if you looked with care, the brick lined fire or heating channel was still apparent. The mill was probably small compared to that of Bulow and may only have produced syrup. There were some depressions in the soil perhaps indicating the position of the needed kettles.

SEARCH FOR THE LOST PLANTATIONS OF FLAGLER COUNTY

Back on the Dupont property I did photograph what appears to me to be a sugar kettle. There were pieces of machinery lying about too.

Hewitt had an old post card that showed an ox or animal powered grinding unit for making sugar syrup. I saw that a piece of old metal lying in the brush seemed to be identical to that pictured as the grinding head in this old card.

Animal powered sugar cane grinders were used on smaller plantations

I saw more pieces of what appeared to be mill machinery. Most had been sold for scrap in World War II. Lying next to a tree and almost embedded into it was a short length of heavy chain, consisting of short and long lengths which could make a conveyer belt to feed raw cane into the mill? Perhaps some of the metal items I photographed were connected to the animal powered mill operation. Hewitt said he doubted that a steam engine was ever here, but animal power could provide enough energy for their needs.

Cut coquina blocks outlined areas that may have been the ruins of the Dupont sugar line.
The gate to the Dupont cemetery was south of

Marineland on A1A and was a narrow dirt road blocked by a combination lock we could not open. This did not stop Hewitt Dupont who took us a bit north of it to the guard house of a gated community.

"I am a Dupont and want to visit my ancestors," he said to the puzzled uniformed guard seeing our large 4-wheel van.

"What street do they live on?"

The guard was confused, but he pressed the gate opener and we drove in, going to a dead end street where a wood might lead to our destination.

Dupont family cemetery photo by Sisco Deen

Here were the graves of Abraham, Benjamin, and Virgil plus many more. On Abraham's stone was a mention of Milton, age 18, who was killed after falling from a horse. This silent spot, rarely visited was only a short distance from the modern homes of a gated community.

Behind the rear fence Hewitt pointed out an area which might be for slave burials, unmarked except for a few broken pieces of coquina rock.

Hewitt Dupont at the stone of his ancestor Virgil Dupont.

Hewitt Dupont recalls lost sections of Old King's Road.

The Dupont family had lived here for a very long time and also remembered the many changes and re-routes of the Old King's road that they had used since they were children. Here too was the location of the Duke Stage Stop and station, forgotten now by most passersby. History is well hidden within the modern part of Flagler County and its growing city of Palm Coast, but there are still a few residents who recall what was here long ago.

Travelling to the Eatman Cemetery, not far from the new Matanzas High School we found what may be one of the oldest grave sites here, that of Mr. Joseph Long who died in an Indian attack at the Dupont plantation in 1836 during the Second Seminole War. Perhaps this is the point to tell some of this story.

Translation from **Florida Herald Issue May 11 1836**
(Wednesday) by Bill Ryan
(original pages faded and difficult to read)
(**Sunday would be May 8, 1836**)

More Indian Murder and depredations -- Mr. Abraham Dupont, who resides at Matanzas about 25 miles south of this city, arrived on Sunday morning about 7 o'clock, having travelled on foot all night with his two little sons, whence he was obliged to flee for safety. Mr. Dupont states that about 10 o'clock on Saturday night he was alarmed by some of his Negroes, who told him that the Indians were at the Negro houses. Mr. Joseph Long who had come over from the opposite side of the River for the purpose of hunting cattle the next day, lodged at Mr. D's house, was roused, and also his children. Mr. Long on arising up, proposed going to the stable to get his horse, and jumped out of the window and proceeded towards the stable when he was shot down about 40 yards from the house. Mr. Dupont had four guns loaded in his house, three of which he fired in the direction of the place where Mr. Long was shot, which had the effect of making the Indians retreat farther off, when they commenced firing at the house and yelling. He was thus enabled to come out of his house by the back door, and fearing his retreat to his boats were cut off, he fled across his field through the thickets to the public road.

Mr. Dupont met some of his Negroes, from whom he procured a blanket and wrapped round one of his children, who had been forced to come away without his clothes. A Negro man belonging to Mr. Dupont, who had been taken by the Indians was with them about six hours, arrived here in the afternoon, states that he went around among the Negro houses, and found them all deserted, with the exception of one old Negro and a small Negro child, and as the Indians showed no disposition to molest the Negroes he left the child in charge of the old Negro. They had ransacked Mr. Dupont's house and loaded his horses with plunder, one of which the Negro brought off with him when he made his escape. They distributed Mr. Dupont's guns among the Ne-

groes and told them to kill every white man they saw. They had previously visited Gen. Hernandez's plantation and secured their Negroes, whom they carried off. The rest of the Negroes escaped to town, as did all the slaves of Mr. Dupont.

On Sunday morning, upon the receipt of the above information, Gen. Scott sent Capt Dunson's Company of U.S. Artillery, unmounted accompanied by 10 volunteers in each of them. After riding until sunset the came upon a party of Indians, 7 to 10 in number, who were driving off a large body of cattle. The volunteers were in advance and charged upon them and fired wounding two of them. The Indians returned the fire and killed Mr. Dupont's horse under him, and wounded Capt Dimick's. The remainders of the Indians fled into the Hammock near by, and were pursued by the troops who then poured in a heavy fire. One of the regulars was killed and four wounded two of them severely - - night coming on they were compelled to retire in the open woods; where they encamped and remained a few hours but as there was no water for horses or men, they retired to St. Josephs.

The Dupont affair would have happened on Saturday May 7th 1836. The Militia certainly rode out to do battle Sunday and returned that evening to St. Augustine. The militia men would not be in a happy frame of mind having lost a friend.

Calvin L. Eatman b 1832 NC, - d 30 Dec 1899 purchased a tract of land known as the Long Grant (5 Sec. 42, 478.42 acres) and built his plantation that included an orange grove and cattle. A family cemetery was established and Mr. and Mrs. Eatman were buried there. Here is also buried Joseph Long who had bravely came to warn the Dupont Plantation of the marauding Indians.

I was fascinated by this image on the Florida Memories web site. "Those are eyes of a Dupont." I said as I looked at this old Dupont photo *(Florida Photographic Collection PR03635)* the history site had not fully identified him listing only as "Joseph Dupont." The image haunted me for he was looking boldly into the future. My life was in photography, and this image was an excellent early Daguerreotype portrait. It was possibly made around the late 1850's. I had printed it out and it was identified as being of Joseph Henry Dupont who was a distant cousin of the Flagler Duponts. Here Joseph was a young man, dressed in his best, ready to meet any challenge of the future.

He was a captain in the Florida Calvary during the War Between the States. Was he a frequent visitor to the Dupont home in the Hammock area? His father Charles H. Dupont was a famous Chief Justice of the Florida Supreme Court.

Sometimes an old photo has the power to bring you to days past, and this is why I like to look at them.

Wikipedia had said this about Charles H. Dupont: "In 1853, his campaign for election as a Florida Supreme Court Justice was successful..." Mr. Dupont was not appointed until 1854 and would have removed himself from any family affairs at law.

The celebrated Hernandez mule killing and the slave Luke case was resolved in 1853 when the Court dismissed the charges on a technicality that the original arrest was made under the wrong law. Much money was spent defending him on principle. I don't think the slave Luke spent any time in jail. Here was a photo of the son of Justice Charles H. Dupont who was also an active planter in Gadsden County and owned more than 100 slaves. He may not have been in favor for any "rights" for a Florida slave especially not to give testimony in a court. Mr. Dupont had a significant legal career in Florida even following the Civil War.

I never cease to be amazed about "synergy," the connection of one event to another that often will happens to you when looking back in time. Some stories are hidden but others will surge forth to say more.

Luke, the mule shooter, will appear again!

8 - Luke Is Baptized

Charles A. Tingley is the Senior Research Librarian at the St. Augustine Historical Society. The library is in an old building on Charlotte Street where researchers sit quietly looking into the past of the "Nation's Oldest City."

I was trying to convince him that the final rest of John Joachim Bulow was next to that of his father's grave in the old Huguenot cemetery. Mr. Tingley knows much about this location. He quickly pulled their microfilm records as we searched for the "death notice" of young Bulow, one that he had located previously with James Fiske of the Flagler County Historical Society.

As the microfilm images flashed up on the screen, a frame appeared with the name Dupont so we halted. Here was a confirmation of baptisms dated May 1855 at the Dupont plantation. Mr. Tingley made a print copy that I quickly emailed to Hewitt. Allene Dupont then spotted a name **Luke**, the slave of Abraham Dupont, the slave who had been part of the celebrated court case.

There were 22 names on the record. Two were definitely male, Luke and Mark, but the remainder appeared to be female. There surely is an interesting story here. Abraham was one of the founders of the Trinity Church in St. Augustine. Now we had this extensive list of mostly females being baptized on the Dupont plantation by the Rev. F.H. Rutlidge and Mr. A.A. Miller, Rector. Certainly the Dupont plantation would be more than a one-day trip from St. Augustine. This was a large, major event at the plantation. The document also noted that they were "servants" of William A. Dupont. Allene Dupont pointed out that William was born in 1839 which would make him only 16 years old in 1855. This remains a mystery. Could a sixteen year old boy be a manager of a plantation? Back then I believe he could. His father Virgil owned the plantation.

Here was Luke being baptized into the Christian world after going thru several years of legal activities on the celebrated Hernandez mule case. Young William Augustus

Dupont will later die from wounds at the battle of Seven Pines in 1862. His name is inscribed on the Confederate monument across the street from the Trinity Church in St. Augustine. Why are these slaves listed as his "servants" in May of 1855? It certainly would be no easy task to travel from St. Augustine to this plantation then occupied by Virgil Dupont, the son of Abraham. I have no answers for you, only my guesses.

I wish that William were here to tell us.

9 - Joseph Marion Hernandez – 1792 to 1857

Joseph Hernandez acquired over 20,000 acres of Florida land some by purchase, some by marriage. He was a man of great reputation both in politics and in the Seminole War where he was a brilliant general of the Militia. He was noted for his plantations in the area of Grahams Swamp called Buena Vista (present day Washington Oaks State Park), Mala Compra (Flagler County Bing's Landing Park), and St. Joseph's (shopping area now in central Palm Coast.)

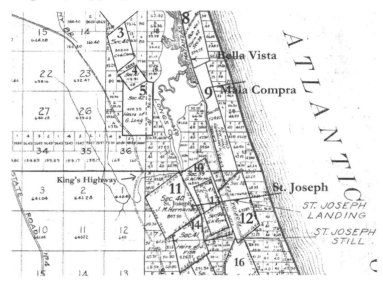

Many historians have collected information on the Hernandez family including Sisco Deen, Dr. Mildred L. Fryman, and observations of Al Hadeed. The MalaCompra site was the center of a great archeological dig. While searching on the 1930 plantation survey map and reading the Hernandez documents I found that some of my fog on the 'lost plantations' began to clear a bit. We certainly were living in a wonderful, historic location now known at Palm Coast and the County of Flagler. The small green building behind the historic Holden House Museum in the small town of Bunnell Florida held some great treasures of information.

Joseph M. Hernandez portrait donated by his great-great-granddaughter Sally Frost Walker French to the Flagler County Historical Society. This was part of four small family oil portraits etched on marble. Portrait is courtesy of Flagler County Historical Society. The Flagler County Historical Society has a unique Hernandez collection donated by family members. Mr. Hernandez was an important personage for Florida and the county of Flagler where he was part of its rich history.

1 January 1836 - the Seminole War had begun

When General Joseph M. Hernandez rode down King's Road with his staff, he halted at his plantations of MalaCompra and St. Joseph's. Onwards to Bulow's he saw the bales of cotton piled up to fortify the Bulow house, and a strong army fort now complete. The army had taken over Bulowville infuriating young Bulow. Hernandez then did several dangerous scouting trips from Bulowville until his departure on the 5th of January 1836 from Bulowville returning to his headquarters in St. Augustine. His staff and escort of 22 soldiers had added to the forces and refugees now at Bulowville. They occupied every building there including many of the slave houses. [29]

Hernandez was 47 years old and certainly knew the Bulow family well, having served as an attorney for them in the purchase of their town house in St. Augustine. I could find no record of his speaking to the very angry young Bulow who certainly did not approve of the army's occupancy.

Remarkably it was observed that Gen. Hernandez never lost the life of any soldiers directly under his command nor took the life of any Native American. [30] All of his captives were taken at sunrise raids with complete surprise so they would surrender. [31] He also had urged the federal government in Washington not to remove the Seminoles from Florida. While he wished to avoid an Indian war, he also believed in being prepared. He had anticipated this Seminole war and requested 500 muskets from Washington, and then organized a defense militia. He was acclaimed as an excellent leader in later hearings given at the US Congress and highly praised by General Putnam.

Later in testimony from a member of his staff, LT. George L. Phillips, it was related that they toured all of Bulow's excellent buildings "in the highest state of repair, and the works in highest order."

Hernandez was an important figure in the history of Florida. He was a successful planter and landowner. He initially acquired 375 acres from Spanish Governor Estrada in 1815. He kept adding more land such as 1,000 acres on Pellicer Creek, 500 acres north of the Picolata River, and then another 500 acres on the Halifax River. His father Martin was a Minorcan settler and was given a Spanish grant land south of Pellicer Creek in the area near the then wreck of the Hewitts sawmill.

Born in 1793 [32] in St. Augustine, he went to school in

Savannah, attends law school in Havana and served as a soldier during the Patriot War when gangs of militia tried to grab Spanish territory for the Americans. He married a wealthy widow, Anna Maria Williams Hill, whom under Spanish law could not retain the property rights of the children's share inherited from their father Samuel Williams plantation owner.

Anna Maria Williams Hill

Anna Maria had four children at her marriage, then ten more with Hernandez. They lived at the Mala Compra Plantation until the Seminole War, and then moved to a home in St. Augustine which was Gen. Hernandez headquarters. When Joseph Hernandez was absent on frequent political and business trips Ana Maria was in charge.

Gen. Hernandez held title to Bella Vista (which would later become the Washington Gardens Park), MalaCompra which was his home and St. Joseph's. These were three important plantations in the history of what is now Flagler County Florida.

He captured Seminole chief King Philip and his party near the Tomoka River, and war leader Osceola south of Moultrie in St. Augustine. The last made some bad publicity as Hernandez had been ordered by his superior Gen. Putnam to ignore a white flag of truce.

When the US took over Florida in 1821, he transferred his allegiance to the United States and served the army from 1835 to 1838 during the worst of the Seminole war. He was the first mayor of St. Augustine, was a delegate to the 17th Congress from the Florida Territory in 1822 to 1823, and ran as a Whig for US Senate in 1845.

He was Florida's first representative in the U.S. Congress

and the first Hispanic to serve. President James Monroe appointed him as the first presiding officer of the Florida Territorial Legislative Council and Hernandez greeted the Americans when they took over Florida in 1821. As a planter, he was the first President of the Florida Agricultural Society

After the war, Hernandez returned trying to re-open his St. Joseph plantation but this was not successful. He died at his family's sugar estate in the District of Coliseo, Matanzas Province, Cuba on June 8, 1857.

Hernandez artifacts were donated to Flagler County Historical Society.

A remarkable collection of Hernandez artifacts were donated to the Flagler County Historical Society including his table ware, wine decanters, soup tureen, engraved color family portraits and many other items from Flagler County's most famous historical figure. Sally Walker French also presented Hernandez etched color portrait display to society members.

These historical images had never before been shown. Hernandez table setting donated by family members was presented at the Holden House museum in Bunnell Florida. They are now displayed at the Flagler County Government Services Building. One wine decanter has a chip, perhaps done when being rapidly packed at the MalaCompra plantation in fear of an Indian attack. These are known as being used by General Hernandez while he was the Florida delegate to the US Congress from 1822 to 1823. Presenting Hernandez artifacts were:

Sally Walker French
Lucia Walker Fairlie Pulgram
Stephanie Burkhalter

Included were dinner plates, decanters with Hernandez crest, serving plate and lid, large china fruit bowl, china serving platter, plus a period pillbox with personal jewelry and pendants of the Hernandez family. These give an excellent look into the fashions used by the wealthy Hernandez family. The framed oil portraits etched onto soft stone are unique.

The Hernandez house in St. Augustine was located on Charlotte Street, not far from the sea wall, near Treasury Street. In 1885 it was a boarding house with 21 rooms and maintained by Mrs. J. V. Hernandez.

The Hernandez display at the Flagler County Government Services building reflects the County's pride held in their first Florida delegate to the U.S. Congress and his rich history

The Hernandez family portraits are rare, colored etchings on stone. They show a younger General Hernandez. They may have been made when he first served in the U.S. Congress.

10 - Hernandez and a Colonial Era Sea Port

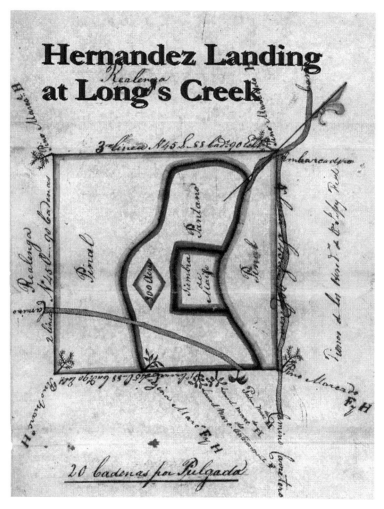

A Spanish land grant paper depicts what local historians believe was a colonial era shipping point for sending sugar, oranges, cotton and dyestuff onto flatboats for transport to sailing ships going to Europe. Known by some as

"Hernandez Landing" and connected to "Long's Creek" this location wound its way northward to the Matanzas River.

To the north of present day Palm Coast, not far from the Old King's highway is the location of a shipping wharf system by which produce from St. Joseph plantation and others could be transshipped to ocean going ships for sale in Europe

Historian Dana Ste.Claire, a life member of the Flagler County Historical Society, guided members to the 800 acre site, which was acquired by the City of Palm Coast, and planned for a park. Historians were amazed at this virtually intact Colonial Era site.

A winding waterway today called Long's Creek connected to the inlet of the Matanzas river and thus a routing to the ocean. Goods could be lightered from a Hernandez built dock. There was a connecting road from the King's Roadway too. The site was shown on old Spanish grant maps and while known by local historians, it was "discovered" and a monetary grant was obtained with the site built as a nature park by the City of Palm Coast. It was recorded as Florida Master Site file 8FL307 with Division of Historical Resources, Tallahassee. [33]

The name of Long's Creek comes from plantation owner Joseph Long who died in the 1836 Indian raid at the Dupont

Plantation.

The shipping area may have reflected the production of the plantations, which included sugar, rum, Sea Island cotton, oranges and juice, indigo, oak timber, and later turpentine or navel stores for shipbuilding. It connected to land grants operated by Hernandez.

The ancient Spanish land grant map was super imposed over a current area map by Mr. Ste. Claire and historian Dot Moore to find an almost exact match for the area identified then as Long's Landing Estuary.

The map showed a bridge pier or embarcadero and a connection to the King's Road. The area also showed many piles of coquina rocks that appeared to be used in buildings, and perhaps some colonial era bricks from a chimney.

"At the most northern point of the peninsula at Long Creek, archaeologists found a raised earthen bulkhead of historically excavated fill that forms a steep bank over Long Creek. Nearby are caches of dressed (cut) coquina stone and other early structural materials. The earthen bulkhead probably supported a wooden wharf during its early operation." 34

Observers noted this site could be placed on the National Registry of Historic locations. It was evident that this "Colonial Era Shipping Port" while perhaps known by a few locals for its beauty, the hunting and fishing potential was a major historic find and should be known as part of the Hernandez legacy in Flagler County.

The city of Palm Coast secured a grant to develop this site. A large parking area and pathways were constructed. At a ribbon cutting I was requested to make some comments on its history with limited time since the focus at that period was on this new and beautiful park.

Historian Al Hadeed had written in a prior memo *"Probably the most important thing to draw attention to this remarkable history is to rename the trail, 'The St. Joseph's Plantation Trail'. It could create a sense of place, a unique bit of history that stimulates conversations or inspiration, art or scholarly study,"* he wrote. 35 (His suggestion was for the main trail through Palm Coast Linear Park which was once part of the St. Joseph's Plantation. If that is not done by the City, it would be appropriate for the City to name the new park trail leading to the historical wharf after the plantation it principally served.)

Since the park was designated as a "nature preserve" its historical aspect was set aside for some future date. City officials observed that historical signage or research would be a "phase two." No time schedule was given.

Normal procedure for listing on the National Register would require a historical study, possibly a consultant and a research into the aspects of the location. It does appear the area contains artifacts from the colonial times and may well be a part of the local heritage.

This is the believed location of the landing where flat boats were loaded with plantation merchandise for shipment to Europe. It may be viewed from a walk way within the new Palm Coast park.

SEARCH FOR THE LOST PLANTATIONS OF FLAGLER COUNTY

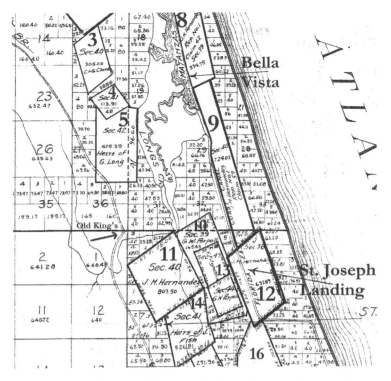

My map shows a Hernandez land grant (11 - section 40 807.50 acres) would extend to touch the headwaters of Long's creek thus offering access to the Matanzas River and eventually access to the Atlantic. Flagler historians hoped that this pristine site of our history will be given future priority for investigation, marked and recorded for visitors to enjoy both its natural beauty and the story of our early entrepreneurs.

This general area was once called as part of Graham's Swamp which contained the rich land observed by early explorers. Thus a Hernandez shipping point would be a logical means to deliver produce to the world market and may have been used by several of the nearby planters.

11 - Hernandez - MalaCompra Plantation

Illustration courtesy Bowman Design Group

"There was a one and a half story framed house on this plantation with a coquina rock foundation three feet deep, and thirty feet long by eighteen wide. The cotton house at Mala Compra was large enough to hold 200,000 pounds of seed and 200 bales of ginned cotton. Among other buildings were a detached kitchen, corn house, cotton house, slave houses, and a driver's house. An extensive grove of sweet oranges and many other trees were on the plantation." In 1999, County Attorney Al Hadeed located old maps and plantation remains. Flagler County obtained grants for $362,000 and an additional $250,000 county grant to research the plantation and prepare an interactive museum within a pavilion at the County's Bing's Landing Park.

Mala Compra - A Plantation in Early Florida
by Sisco Deen

Plantations lined the banks of tidal waterways and freshwater rivers in northeast Florida by the late 1700's. Planters sought wealth from rice and indigo and later Sea Island cotton.

Florida's Spanish government offered free ownership of land to settlers after ten years of homesteading.

Repeated raids and invasions destroyed most homesteaded plantations. Josiah Dupont and then Miguel Crosby owned Mala Compra (Spanish for Bad Bargain.)

When Joseph and Ana Maria Hernandez purchased the plantation in 1816, they could not know that later events would prove the appropriateness of the name and continue the cycle of struggle, loss and abandonment.

Mala Compra was one of the barrier island plantations. The waters of the Atlantic Ocean washed its eastern shore, on the west, the saltwater Matanzas River. These waterways offered the best way to travel among the Hernandez properties and to St. Augustine where a variety of goods were available and religious services, festivals, and political rallies were held.

Flagler attorney and historian Al Hadeed at dedication

Just a few feet below the soil where the crops were planted are layers of coquina (compressed shell stone) easily used to build the walls and foundations of houses and fortifications. The coquina ruins of Mala Compra have fascinated passersby for over 165 years.

 Archeologists discovered two plantation buildings, and found artifacts related to daily activities of Hernandez's time. In spite of previous modern activity, they found artifacts related to food, clothing, and personal items, household and structural items and labor related tools.

The coquina ruins of the building foundations were still visible in an 1818-plat map showing the original building locations. Archaeologists cleared debris from the ruins and excavated the soil around them.

The building ruins also appeared on a 1944 coastal map.

A detailed description of the plantation was found among the Second Seminole War claims in Congressional Records. Historic documents tell us that the main house was 30 by 18 feet with a 10-foot piazza (porch) on one side. A tabby and coquina foundation supported a one and a half story house with a shingled roof. There were 16 shuttered windows, 9 paneled doors and wooden floors.

The house had 6 rooms with plaster walls and a staircase and a brick and coquina double fireplace. Archaeologists actually found a larger building than described with coquina and the fireplaces and some tabby (oyster shell concrete) floors. Excavation showed on tabby floor over another, suggesting an earlier structure beneath the 1816 dwelling. Postholes were found on the west side of the house that may relate to a porch with the piazza to the east.

Evidence of the house included thousands of early machine made nails, a few earlier handmade nails and hand blown window glass. A cellar contained hundreds of bottle fragments and some whole bottles. Was it a wine cellar?

Other lost possessions found 165 years later included bone and shell buttons, medicine jars and bottles, pieces of ceramics and fragments of clay smoking pipes. A Spanish silver coin dated 1810 was also found. Flooring suggests that an earlier smaller structure was incorporated into the Hernandez residence. Here was the house of Josiah Dupont, who had settled the area earlier but abandoned due to Seminole raids.

Weapon related artifacts included gunflints, lead shot, and part of a Spanish flintlock pistol, found in the main house. A well-worn doorsill is still in place. Wall debris and one fireplace indicate that portions of the building were white washed. The other fireplace in the main house was lined with red tiles.

Experts have used early maps, historical descriptions and excavations to piece together what Mala Compra plantation was like in the early 19th century. Using shovels and small trowels, archaeologists, with the help of community volunteers, carefully removed thin layers of soil. They sifted it for artifacts and mapped and photographed color changes seen in the layers.

1998-99 work emphasized exposing the building remains. In 2001, work focused on the search for other cultural features and artifacts. All artifacts were bagged according to location, and then taken to the laboratory for analysis.

While archaeologists and volunteers worked on Mala Compra, historians conducted background research on Joseph Hernandez and his era.

The walls of a substantial coquina well stand undamaged at Mala Compra, but portions above ground have been rebuilt. The part below the ground is original. It is between the main house and the kitchen. South of the kitchen-building archaeologists found a dense trash deposit and a demolished outbuilding or work area. Almost 3000 artifacts were collected there.

A historic account described a 1 ½ frame building on a stone foundation measuring 18 by 30 feet. It had 9 windows, 3 doors, plastered walls, two fireplaces, and a baking oven. The upper room was used to cure tobacco; the lower rooms were a kitchen and a laundry room.

Archaeologists found a building with the approximate dimensions that included two rooms, a double hearth and a possible oven. A tabby floor remains in the laundry room. The kitchen building had a poured tabby floor outside the eastern side that may have been a covered porch or a patio. It was grooved to drain water away from the building.

The main house and the kitchen were built of wood, supported by shaped coquina blocks and tabby mortar. Tabby was a popular concrete-like building material in early Florida composed of lime, sand, oyster shell and water. It could be made into walls, bricks or floors.

Coquina is a local type of limestone formed of tiny shells cemented together. It comes from the Anastasia Formation and is between 12,000 and 2 million years old. It lies beneath the barrier islands between St. Augustine and Melbourne. At Mala Compra natural formations of coquina lie less than five feet below the surface.

Kitchen utensils found included a large pot handle, spoon fragments and a knife blade. Numerous animal bone fragments were recovered in the kitchen yard. The bones are food remains. Their diet included beef, pork, sheep or goat, and chicken, supplemented with fish, alligator and other wild species.

Mala Compra grew Sea Island cotton that offered longer, stronger fibers than short-staple cotton, grown throughout the south. It required many more hours of labor to harvest, clean and pack.

Ownership of plantations and a large work force place Hernandez in the planter class. Planters identified themselves with their plantations. Hernandez referred to himself as "of Mala Compra."

Planter families were considered members of the highest social class. They held political offices, influenced voters, and served as militia officers. They were expected to be gracious hosts. Hernandez invited the naturalist John Audubon to visit, Audubon immortalized Mala Compra in his illustration of the American coot, which he found "in every ditch, bayou and pond" on the plantation.

Audubon considered Hernandez a provincial Spaniard and Hernandez believed Audubon as an uncouth backwoodsman engaged in a useless quest.

Dorotea Hernandez

Ana Maria Williams Hernandez brought 4 children to her marriage with Joseph Hernandez and then had ten more. The Williams children were: William, Samuel, Eliza Ann, and John Theophilus. The Hernandez children were: Ana Eduarda Teresa – b. 1814, Ellen Justa Rupina –b. 1817, Fernando Martin Valentin –b. 1821, Martin Edwardo –b. 1822, Lucia Catalina –b. 1823, Jose Mariano –b. 1825, Maria Josepha –b. 1829 (sic), John Gaspar, Dorotea Frederica Ignacia, and Jose Tomas.

Ana Maria Hernandez was already familiar with plantation life along the saltwater "rivers" south of St. Augustine. She had learned the role of plantation mistress while married to her first husband. Upon his death, she was responsible for keeping the plantations working and profitable – and for trying to protect them against Indian raids.

As a plantation mistress, Ana Maria Hernandez assumed the duty to provide clothing, health care and food for the plantation residents – the family, visitors and many workers. Curing, pickling and otherwise preserving food grown on the plantation required much of her time.

When Joseph Hernandez was absent with frequent political and business responsibilities, Ana Maria was in charge. The life of a planter's wife was hard work – seldom a life of parties and luxury portrayed in television shows or movies.

Enslaved laborers of African descent worked at Hernandez's plantations. In 1832, his slaves ranged from one-month-old Lawrence to 65-year-old Lucy. They planted cotton in March and harvested in the hot days of August, continuing into October. During bad weather, they worked indoors cleaning the cotton. Workers were moved from one Hernandez enterprise to another as needed.

An overseer, William Broadnax, supervised work at Mala Compra and across the river at St. Joseph. Daily work was managed by a driver, who reported to the overseer. Drivers were usually blacks and might be either slave or free.

Cotton plantations sometimes used the task system. When the assigned task was finished, laborers could hunt, fish, or tend their own small cotton crop. Planters allowed a day in the spring for slaves to plant and a day in the fall to harvest the crop, which they sold and kept the profits.

In 1837, twelve of the slaves' houses were made of "wood posts and wattle." Wattle is a method of construction using slender branches and saplings interwoven with poles. Two others were of wooden clapboards and had palmetto frond roofs. There was a wooden privy nearby.

An 1818 survey depicted the workers' houses in two rows at right angles to each other. The driver's house, built of coquina, might have been at the intersection of the two rows. This would have placed the overseer at the head of each row, symbolizing his higher rank among the workers.

The United States and the Seminoles made a series of treaties. A big problem with the agreements was that the Seminoles had no single strong leader. Some chiefs would support a treaty while others denounced it.

In 1800, a Black militia detachment was headquartered at Mala Compra, and then owned by Josiah Dupont, to ward off Indian attacks. After they withdrew to Fort Matanzas, a famous Indian raid happened here. In 1802, Josiah Dupont returned home to Mala Compra to find Seminoles in war paint. The Indians took 10 horses, 4 Negroes and all the household goods they could carry.

Murders of soldiers on Dec. 28, 1835, marked the beginning of the Second Seminole War, or the Florida War, as it was called at the time. General Hernandez commanded the militia units in East Florida.

Plantations in coastal Florida were abandoned, including Mala Compra, and residents fled to St. Augustine and further north.

The Army and Militia occupied rural plantations that were damaged by fighting or modified for defense. Officers were quartered in the manor house at Mala Compra and it may have been a briefing station for detachments heading south. It was also a holding place for slaves recaptured from the Seminoles. St. Joseph, one of Hernandez's other plantations, was the main military depot for the entire region south of St. Augustine.

Mala Compra and St. Joseph were occupied and abandoned several times by troops. As the Seminoles moved northward, both were destroyed.

Hernandez claimed $99,000 in losses resulting from the war. The loss of crops and livestock, expense of supporting slaves unable to work the plantation, damages to several buildings, his orange groves and cotton gins at Mala Compra totaled $9,951." (From a paper prepared by Sisco Deen.)

The MalaCompra Plantation is now recorded on the National Register of Historic Places by the Flagler County Historical Society. Many of the artifacts located in the dig were displayed at the Flagler County Public library. A few are now shown at the Flagler Beach Museum. The site is located in the Bing's Landing Park of Flagler County at 5862 North Oceanshore Blvd.

12 - Bella Vista Plantation Now A State Park

Image Washington Oaks State Park signage

The original site of Washington Oaks State Park (8 - sec 39) may lie on British John Moultrie's land when he was lieutenant governor of British Florida. Moultrie called the site Bella Vista in the 1760's. It contained an orange grove. In 1802, a new owner, Juan Baptista Ferreyra, appeared. In 1818 his son sold his father's grant to Joseph M. Hernandez. Washington Oaks was owned by the Hernandez family for seven decades. They also called this land "Bella Vista." It became part of Hernandez extensive land holdings and acquisitions.

In 1845 Hernandez's daughter Luisa (Lucia Catalina) married George Lawrence Washington, a distant relative of the first President of the United States. George practiced law and resided with Luisa and their family in St. Augustine. In August of 1877, Dorothea Hernandez Walker purchased Bella Vista as part of the Hernandez estate. In the 1870's George had acquired some of the land from the Hernandez estate and constructed an hunting and fishing lodge, dug two artesian wells, planted citrus groves and built a dock on the river.

Hernandez was an active agriculturalist and made

experiments in the cultivation of sugar cane, which may have occurred on Bella Vista. His property was located on the Matanzas River which gave good access to ocean going ships.

He was known to raise crops of cotton and sugar cane although there is no record of sugar production at Bella Vista.

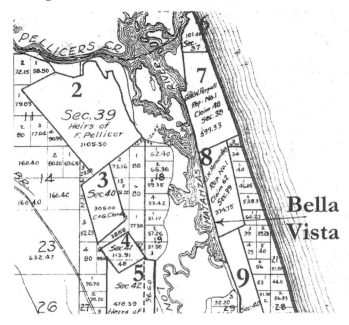

Prior to the Seminole War, it appears Hernandez was having some financial pressure and had heavily mortgaged his properties. Later his estate sold much of his land holdings.

The property was then called "The Washington Place." The beautiful Washington Oaks Park went through a series of owners after George L. Washington acquired it in the mid-1870 It was later planned to become a massive development called Hernandez Estates in 1926 but was cancelled by the financial collapse of the depression and end of the Florida land boom.

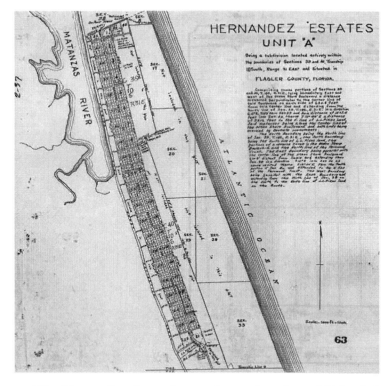

The Young family took over in 1936 and established the name "Washington Oaks" plus extensive gardens. They did much to expand and maintain the property. The land was donated after his death and became a Florida State Park on July 1 1964.

The stately live oak trees at Washington Oaks State Gardens Park certainly existed in the time of Gen. Hernandez and his ownership of the land. It was considered in the same era as MalaCompra plantation in terms of his growing crops here. These ancient trees almost certainly existed even back to the times of British occupation before the American Revolution. Decorated with hanging Spanish moss they tell the story of our Lost Plantations to anyone who will pause, meditate and consider our rich history.

BellaVista is no longer, but its trees remain with us

Searching for St. Joseph's Plantation

In the 1960s a local Boy Scout troop and amateur historians began to investigate St. Joseph's plantation ruins. One of Florida's great plantations still held many showing artifacts in what would later become a major shopping area in the new City of Palm Coast. (Images are from collection of Robert Creal Flagler Beach Historical Society.) Hernandez had attempted to restart his St. Joseph's operation after the Seminole War and reportedly was producing 3000 gallons of syrup and 300 hogsheads of raw sugar by 1850. [36] The attempt was later a failure and the property abandoned.

St. Joseph's Plantation – Lost and Forgotten

In a busy Palm Coast shopping center that is bounded by Old King's Road, Palm Coast Parkway and Florida Park Drive North rests some of the unmarked memory of a great and historic sugar plantation called St. Joseph's. The name of the road in the area before Palm Coast development was St. Joe Grade and there was a St. Joe shopping center several miles from the plantation. (later there was a turpentine operation in the early 1900s operated by D.D. Moody, who knew the area well as a surveyor.) St. Joseph plantation was part of a complex of properties owned and developed by Joseph M. Hernandez including those of Bella Vista (now Washington Gardens), and Mala Compra plus many other smaller land grants and developments. By the 1820s it was reportedly in full production and in the 1830's the Hernandez family was living at MalaCompra.

In 1834 the Hernandez properties were heavily mortgaged, he had borrowed monies to continue and expand. A step-son, John T. Williams was engaged as plantation manager. Thus it was a financial disaster when the Second Seminole War began in December of 1835 and in February of 1836 his plantation was named as Camp Brisbane and occupied by soldiers. Sometime in February of 1836 the plantation was burned and destroyed by the Seminole Indians.

Early in the days of the Palm Coast city development, ICDC* construction engineers found the remains of the floor of an immense sugar mill, said to be the largest on the Florida East Coast, commonly called the St. Joe sugar mill after its owner, General Joseph Hernandez of St. Augustine. The State of Florida in approving the development of Palm Coast required ITT to document the historic resources in a report[37] but allowed the developer to destroy and fill-in the historic ruins. ICDC asked some of the then County Commissioners to visit the site to tell them if it had any lasting historical significance. Reportedly, the commissioners said it was a pile of useless rocks and so advised the ICDC planners. As a result, fill dirt dredged from finger canals were put over the plantation ruins, to all intents and purposes St. Joseph sugar mill was obliterated.

The ICDC engineers hadn't reckoned on the enterprise of historical minded Circuit Judge Billy Wadsworth. In deciding to live at Palm Coast, Judge Wadsworth displayed his usual wisdom by picking what he believed to be the old site of the St. Joe sugar mill. The house he bought in the 1970's had a little canal frontage, but the lot next door was vacant so he bought it, too. Then he started digging for a patio floor and found one, already made of coquina boulders. It was the floor of the old sugar mill he had uncovered. [38]

*A construction/engineering firm for Palm Coast.

The St. Joseph's plantation was frequently mentioned during the Second Seminole War, which began on Christmas of 1835 as it was a place of refuge for frightened refugees, and wounded soldiers. Federal troops occupied it in February 1836 calling it Camp Brisbane, a field hospital. Sometime after this the Seminoles burned the abandoned works. In 1842 Hernandez tried to re-establish St. Joseph's. His first crop was poor due to a wet season, but by 1850 he was reportedly yielding 3,000 gallons of syrup, and 300 hogsheads of sugar. [39]

In 1856 he abandoned his efforts and moved to Cuba.

GENERAL JOSEPH M. HERNANDEZ AND ST. JOSEPH'S PLANTATION

By Eileen H. Butts - Volusia County Record
(Flagler Historical Society files)

"Joseph M. Hernandez born in St. Augustine, 1786, of Minorcan parents, was well-known and respected in Spanish Florida, being the most distinguished coastal planter of his time. He was schooled in Savannah from the age of fifteen and thence went to Havana to read law, returning to St. Augustine in 1811 where he took up legal practice.

He was quickly accepted by the plantation gentry and other aristocracy, making an excellent position for himself by his industry, native intelligence and by a most auspicious marriage with Anna Maria Hill, beautiful and wealthy widow of Samuel Williams, Esq., whose plantation, .'Orange Grove," was located on land that was purchased by Matthias Day in 1870. The Williams grant formed the nucleus of what was to become Daytona. When in 1821 Florida came under the American flag,

Hernandez transferred his citizenship from Spain to the United States and by 1822 was appointed by President Monroe to the first Legislative Council, being named by Monroe "one of the thirteen most fit and discreet men of the territory." Almost immediately thereafter he was elected by the territory as its first delegate to congress, taking his seat in the second session of the 17th Congress at the age of thirty-five. Another honor bestowed on him was that of President of the Agricultural Society of St. Augustine, a position his experience as a very large and important land owner had qualified him to fill. He had property both in St. Augustine and in the area not too distant. The three chief plantations were Bella Vista, Mala Compra (Bad Bargain), and St. Joseph's, all bordering the Matanzas for five or six miles south of Pellicer Creek.

Today, the ruins of the St. Joseph sugar mill are on property that has recently been purchased by a land development company. These beautiful and unusual ruins are in a series of levels running down a hillside that extends nearly two hundred and fifty feet.

In A. J. Hanna's book; Florida's Golden Sands St. Joseph is described as follows: "Its fields were scientifically drained by canals from five and seven feet wide, with identical depths and from one-half mile to one and one-half miles in length. Two hundred acres were cross-ditched with ditches two feet wide and two deep and separated by a distance of thirty-five feet. Causeways, bridges and road completed this ambitious project.

'The coquina-rock sugar curing house at St. Joseph's was sixty-seven feet by thirty-one with division walls, cemented and plastered for four molasses cisterns. This house was connected with a coquina-rock boiling house, forty-one by thirty-two feet, arranged for two sets of kettles; these were four double and two single coolers made of white pine. Two double receivers with a capacity of 750 gallons conveyed the raw juice from the mill to the receivers.

The engine house was thirty by twenty feet and twenty-five high; its equipment included one ten-horsepower rotary-valve engine and boiler and one horizontal roller mill for grinding cane. St. Joseph's was considered "the most valuable plantation soil wise, in Florida," by a former Bahaman sugar planter who described it in the Farmer's Register of 1835. "Hernandez had with great perseverance and success overcome the laborious difficulties of clearing and draining new land, and has under culture upwards of 200 acres of these swamp lands." The judgment of this observer was that the swamp-lands of East Florida and especially those lying on the branches of the Matanzas and Halifax Rivers are superior in strength and character for the production or sugar to the most valued lands of the West India Islands.

During the Seminole War, Hernandez was named Brigadier General and mustered a brigade of militia for the purpose of protecting St. Augustine and Jacksonville and the settlements along the St. Johns River. Later, his military activities brought him the only blot upon his otherwise splendid record. His capture of Coacoochee and Osceola under a flag of truce however was not done with his approval but has been established as an order given him by his superior General Jesup.

However, so great was the destruction of the plantations of East Florida by the Seminoles, few were ever reestablished, particularly as the United States Government lowered the tariff in sugar from the West Indies. Many of our most successful planters drifted away and the greatly honored and beloved Joseph Hernandez joined the exodus returning to Cuba in the late 1840's or early 1850's--where he died and was buried in Matanzas June 1856."

Image by Robert Creal – Flagler Beach Historical Society

The St. Joseph enterprise of Gen. Hernandez has vanished. The intersections of Palm Coast Parkway, Florida Park Drive and Old King's road are some of the busiest in the modern Palm Coast community, but virtually no one is aware they are passing one of the largest sugar plantation works in Florida as not a whisper of it remains.

Spanish Mission? Hernandez picked an interesting name "St. Joseph's" for his plantation. The Spanish had been in Florida for some 200 years prior. They did build a series of missions including one called "San Josef de Jororo." (Osceola County) Because the early plantation ruins had such a "Spanish look" many locals theorized that there were missions perhaps at Bulowville and at St. Joseph's. One researcher John A. Gallant wrote Florida State University in March of 1964 as follows:

"I first heard of the site from D.D. Moody, Flagler County's Tax Assessor and a surveyor there for nearly 40 years. He told me he had first seen it in the early 1920's while running a survey, and a few years later took the late Jeannette Thurber (Mr.S. Washington) Connor there. He recalls that she had a list of three missions to the Jororo built in the 1690's, together with their exterior dimensions, and the Flagler ruin fitted almost exactly her description for San Josef." [40]

He enclosed his findings, and artifacts located. The Florida State experts called them 18th to late 19th Century and not from the Spanish period.

He had enclosed a detail report plus an area that did not appear to be the same as the other Plantation ruins. During the ITT Palm Coast development Charles Waterman wrote a paper in August 1 1953 saying the Hernandez grant was on the site of a Jesuit mission, St. Joseph.

In the 1950's several archaeologists including John W. Griffin wrote that the possibility of Spanish Missions in Flagler or Volusia Counties did not exist. Articles and papers were written stating the Spanish had no missions in this area. However, D. D. Moody and others were convinced there were missions present.

Within the shopping areas of Palm Coast there are no historical markers or information at to what was once there. These too have grown old and are now being replaced by newer stores and shops.

Over the years and during construction several historical groups requested that the Hernandez plantation site be identified and marked. The Boy Scout dig was some 54 years ago and only a four page incomplete report rests in the files of the Flagler Historical Society as a record of their effort.

13 - We Live In a Different World

"Today we live in a world of developers who want a "natural Florida" that fits into their idea of what Florida should be, not the real natural Florida," Sisco Deen Florida native and historian.

Would that there exists a time machine that could reveal the labors of planting, building structures, houses, barns, establishing herds of cattle, the skill of slaves who created much of this. What stories of adventure and enterprise could be told.

In Florida today we find the plans of the land developer, new homes for those moving from the cold of northern states to a warmer climate. We no longer know of an Industrial Revolution that once began here so long ago. In the early Florida wilderness existed vast plantations with laboring steam engines, crushing mills for valuable sugar works, and shipment of finished products to England, France and Spain for a new world economy. We had the evil of slave labor, yet perhaps it differed from our modern perceptions.

Here deep in these once busy fields lie pieces of broken pottery. They can tell us that once there were even older enterprises, Indian towns or villages existing here perhaps many thousands of years ago. Pieces of broken pottery that may be older than the 3,150 B.C., days of ancient Egypt can be found. What a story they must hold! They tell us of man's ingenuity and his desire to create. Wait, I said "man" but the ancient Indians were a matriarchal society. Women were in charge!

These ancient Indians lived in villages, in towns that existed when Rome was a world power, when the Egyptians built the pyramids. They speak of a technology and people about whom we know very little, yet they too lived here harvesting the beds of oysters that grew here, enjoying the beautiful sea shore and the warm climate of what would later be called Florida The markings on old maps give us only a hint of what enterprise grew here, but is surely these were stories of struggle, promise and effort to make a life in

"Florida."
Our past stories fade rapidly. Old maps, digitized Spanish grant documents, and the vanishing stories of Florida natives rarely remain as Florida's rapid development alters the face of this land.

*Broken ancient pottery tells its story at the **Flagler Beach Museum**.*

Palo Indian 8,000 B.C.+ years
Early Archaic 7,000-5000
Middle Archaic 5,000-3,000
Late Archaic 3,000-2,000
Late Archaic 2,000 (Orange)

14 - The Florida Past

The ancient ones – The early Indians

Large numbers of early Indians once lived in east Florida. They were sometimes named as Timucua. By the time of Columbus, it was estimated that some 900,000 were living in Florida and South East Georgia. Here were the Apalachee (Tallahassee), Ais (Cocoa), Calusa (Ft. Meyers), Jaega (Ft. Lauderdale), Mayaimi (Lake Okeechobee), Timuca (here), and Tocobaga (Tampa).

The Europeans had made slaves of these early people, killed them, or forced them to accept Christianity and the culture of Europe. The Timucua had almost vanished by 1717 due to imported European diseases and warfare. Huge piles of discarded shells called middens mark their history. A large shell pile of these ancient ones once existed to the north of what would later become the Bulow plantation. These shell piles were found to be useful by the British era settlers in building their roadways and even by 'modern' Florida road builders. The early Indian groups had existed in Florida for thousands of years. They were documented by amazed explorers as to "their size and impressive appearance" when compared by the early Spanish and French explorers who were of shorter stature.

The early Indians were said to live in walled villages in the interior of Florida in the winter and move to the more pleasant seashore in the summer. The areas around the Tomoka and Halifax rivers were rich sites of these early Indian villages. A few surviving Timucuan Indians had remained to depart with the Spaniards to Havana when the British arrived. Others were captured by new immigrating tribes of Indians and sold to the English for slaves in northern colonies.

The once powerful Timucuan ceased to exist as a race by the late 1700's. Their shell mounds were their only record. The mounds later became a much-used building resource in surfacing the British King's Road built prior to the American Revolution.

A fine collection of Indian pottery exists at the Flagler Beach, Florida Historical Museum. It reflects the thousands of years of living in Florida, a people and a culture now long vanished. Many ancient Indian sites existed in Flagler County.

Marvel at the ages past in the pottery exhibit.

15 - Many Flags and Many People

History involves the actions of real people, their desires, and their response to events of the time. It is often difficult to separate our history into dates or "periods" as historical happenings may flow along one single lifetime or extend into a family history of grandfather, father, sons and daughters. We can read about those who lived, fought and died in a difficult land, often in desperate times, but only our imagination can say what their lives might have been. Events of the many years prior can have a direct effect on happenings of much later times. To understand the history of Florida you need to know some of the events that happened in times past. Here is a brief description of those that came to early Florida.

French arrive in Florida

In June of 1564, an expedition sailed from France under the command of Rene de Laudonniere and made their approach to the **River of Dolphins**, their name for the present harbor of St. Augustine in consequence of the large number of dolphins observed by them at its mouth.

They afterwards coasted to the north, and entered the River St. Johns, called by them the **River May**. [41] They built a fort and colony called **Fort Caroline**. It was near the present day Jacksonville. However, on August 28, 1565, Spanish Menendez de Aviles arrived in Florida to establish a new colony they would name St. Augustine. He carried instructions from King Philip II of Spain to destroy the French Protestant Huguenots. On September 20, 1565, his force went overland to arrive at Fort Caroline during a storm.

The French fort was taken and after a great killing it was renamed San Mateo. This was the end of the French venture in Florida. French ships had also been blown south; either sunk or wrecked on the Florida sands by the storm. The soldiers of Menendez killed the shipwrecked survivors. Only a few survived to tell the story. The area of the massacre is called Matanzas for "bloody slaughter." The river bore this name to this date.

Spanish settle St. Augustine 1565 to 1763

Spanish explorers had reached Florida as far back as 1512, and perhaps even earlier. Juan Ponce de Leon reached the northeast coast, and many expeditions followed. The first lasting settlement was that of Pedro Menendez de Aviles in 1565 when he set his colony at St. Augustine. Spain then held Florida for some 198 years.

St. Augustine was mostly a military encampment, trying to survive attacks, pirate raids, violent storms and frequent lack of support by the mother country. The Spanish lifeline remained the rich treasure galleons sailing north following the Gulf Stream, taking the dangerous route from Mexico to Spain. St. Augustine was a port of security for shipwrecked sailors and possible protection for Spanish commerce.

Spain held Florida against great adversity, attacks by pirates and British soldiers until 1763 when the British took over following the Treaty of Paris. The Spanish had to depart with many sailing to Havana. Only a few settlers remained in Florida. The British arrived to find a much-reduced St. Augustine now lacking enough population to make a viable town.

16 - Slaves Escape into Florida.

A ride for liberty - Eastman Johnson, courtesy Brooklyn Museum

"In the early days of our country, the road to freedom extended to the South and into the wilds of Florida instead of to the North. The road we now call as Old Kings could be a useful route of escaping slaves." *William Ryan presentation paper to National Underground Railroad Conference, St. Augustine 2012*

I had observed that the early Spanish at first had encouraged slave escape from the British colonies to the north of Florida. Escapes during the 1730's continued even under the more restrictive British occupation of Florida. Slaves still arrived to conceal themselves in the wilds of Florida, sometimes in association with Indian settlements. Small 'freedom' villages were scattered across Florida. Slave escape to Florida continued into the Second Spanish period when the Spanish under great pressure had agreed to return escaped slaves.

Florida thus remained a refuge for slaves who might flee from the harsh plantation life in Georgia, or the Carolinas. The Spanish king, in order to twist the British Lion's tail, even adopted a fugitive slave policy of 1693 offering freedom to those slaves that could reach Florida and would declare their allegiance to him and to the Catholic Religion. Escapees were baptized into the Catholic faith. [42]

The Spanish had slaves too, but their legal code was much different from what would occur in the much more restrictive rules later in the British and American rule of Florida. Under the Spanish code, a slave had certain rights as a human being and the right to petition if unfairly treated. The later fierce 'Slave Laws' of the new United States happened after 1821, were a direct reaction to the rumors and the actuality of free escaped slaves who had lived in Florida for over a hundred years.

In numbers, these free former slaves were not many, but the concept of losing valuable workers was ever a sore point to the plantation owners in the Georgia, Carolina and other colony areas. These events will have a dramatic effect on Florida Plantations although they would not happen until many years later with the beginning of the Second Seminole War. The wilds of Florida had concealed escaping slaves for many years. Often the escapees were in a relationship with the Florida Indians. Being good builders, farmers, or able to speak languages made them desirable to the Florida Seminole Indians who were themselves escapees into Florida from wars to the North. Escaping slaves did form small communities many on the West Coast of Florida. Their existence was well hidden.

The Slavery that existed in Florida during the early Spanish days thus had a different texture than that which arose after the young United States took over Florida in 1821. The Spanish enlisted Africans in the Spanish Militia and in 1738 built a fort called Gracia Real de Santa Teresa de Mose (Fort Mose) manned by African American freedmen. It was the first free black settlement in the New World. A bloody battle was fought at Fort Mose in 1740 to protect the Spanish settlement from the British. A 1769 census of St. Augustine showed a population of some 1592 residents that included 483 slaves and 102 free Negroes. [43]

Free black men were an important part of the Spanish colonial scene in St, Augustine where they held many of the trade arts and crafts, the baker, the butcher, the candle maker.

British control Florida in 1763

 After one of the many European wars with their shifting alliances, Spain lost Florida and the British took over. Spain had to trade Florida in order to retain its ownership of Cuba. When the British arrived, St. Augustine was almost deserted.

The concept of escaped slaves living in Florida would also become an annoyane to the British and the new United States following its revolution against England 1775 to 1783. The return of 'escaped slaves' in Florida remained a hot issue.

Florida was a wild place and a refuge for many trying to escape the wars and turmoil this new world. These refugees often had association with the Seminoles and also created many small villages along the shore of Florida's Gulf coast where trading and contact with Spanish fishermen from Cuba was possible.

Florida now had a mixture of races, cultures and peoples from every nation who sought freedom in its wilderness.

Abraham was an important interpreter for the Seminoles. 44

New Indian groups had entered Florida. These were from different tribes sometimes called "Creeks" who were chased into Florida by the many wars affecting life to the north. Indian groups would form a close relationship with the escaped slaves some of whom would later be called "Black Seminoles." They adopted the dress and culture of the Indians. Indian leaders also would purchase slaves. "Seminole" was a title given to Indian refugees by the white man. It was "Cimarron" by the Spanish as it meant refugee, stranger or wanderer. Later these new refugees would adopt this title to describe themselves although they had differing languages and cultures.

The escaped former plantation workers might have construction skills, or speak English. Some such as Abraham were skillful in the white man's world and would become interpreters between the Indians and the settlers.

The Seminoles owned slaves too but the relationship and work rules were far different from those on the plantations in Georgia or the Carolinas. The Seminoles held large cattle herds and some of the very first "cow boys" were former slaves now herding Seminole cattle. They followed African traditions of raising cattle.

Florida now had many of the wild former Spanish cattle that escaped during the early Spanish period, prospered in Florida and was there for anyone who could capture and contain them.

Photo courtesy of Florida Agricultural Museum Flagler County.

Cattle thrived in Florida. They resisted disease and soon the Seminoles accumulated large herds. Herds of these 'scrub' cattle were an important trade in Florida and part of the trading between the many planters and the Indian cattlemen. The Agricultural Museum in Flagler County has displays that show the first 'cowboys' as being African slaves in Florida who had a long tradition of cattle management.

Ancestors of Spanish horses sometimes called 'Marsh Tacky" lived here and drive the small, often multi-colored Spanish cattle controlled by long leather whips. The cowmen were later called "crackers" a name that stuck in Florida legend.

H. n.º 22.

Florida

Concesion hecha en 18 de Noviembre de 1817 á favor de D.ⁿ Jose Mariano Hernandez de 20000 acres de tierra en los

Land grants under the second Spanish period exceeded 900

17 - What Might Have Been?

"The plantation economy of the area that developed into Flagler County actually discouraged the formation of concentrated settlements. Large tracts of land were concentrated in the hands of a relative few, introduced gangs of slave laborers, purchased expensive mechanical equipment, and constructed mills, resources and slave quarters." *WPA Spanish Land Grants. Schene, Hopes, pg 30 Tallahassee 1941* [45]

What would our portion of Florida look like today had not the Seminoles declared war in 1835 resulting in the destruction of these vast enterprises and the eventual near depopulation of Florida? Would this industrial economy have remained and evolved into something even greater?

It was a slavery based economy that vanished almost overnight. What remained was only an echo of what was first. I wish I knew more about the human stories of these enterprises. I believe they were built and perhaps operated by those having African ancestors.

If those plantations had remained, what would be Florida today?

The desperate Seminole conflict lasted for seven years and destroyed these great enterprises, scattering the workers and changing their lives.

In my book called *"Osceola His Capture and Seminole Legends"* I told a story of the efforts made by the Florida Seminoles to avoid this disastrous war. I had Osceola tell his story in the first person speaking English to our reader, which in real life he could not do. I do believe it is accurate, although many have pondered how I could have written it. I have found that many stories of old Florida wish to be told and will appear if you listen.

The Seminoles certainly played their role in these now lost and vanished plantations.

In July of 1978 the company of ITT wished to develop these lands that would be called Palm Coast within Flagler

County. They financed *Palm Coast Cultural Resource Assessment,* a study and document by James J. Miller. It appeared to list the early Plantations in the county but concentrated mainly on those that would fall within the new development of Palm Coast. It did not say much about what these enterprises were or what became of them.

Many of these plantations in Flagler County then appeared "lost" or at least forgotten until Sisco Deen's old map gave us some clues at the Flagler County Historical Society.

The **1926 survey map by Goold T. Butler C.E.** shows land grants within Flagler County I have inserted numbering on this map to correspond to the *Palm Coast Cultural Resource Assessment* report that had listed 21 approved grants. The Butler map shows more grants than this. Perhaps the western Flagler grants did not fall within the plans of the new Palm Coast development when the Resource Assessment document was written. The map was scanned by County Clerk Gail Wadsworth's office and I hope later can be available in on line. Land grants were often sold or assigned to others while properties like the later Dupont's were purchased or do not appear at all. This 1926 map was too large to show on these book pages. I am repeating sections of it for you to locate its listed plantations. The original map is at the Flagler County Historical Society.

Good maps of our Colonial Heritage are rare. The Butler

map gives us a good start point in trying to penetrate the haze of history. Who was here and what did they do?

I was launched on a search to look back many years beyond our present rich gated communities, rapidly developing Palm Coast and a Flagler County Florida that today does not resemble what was once here.

Plantation grants in Flagler County

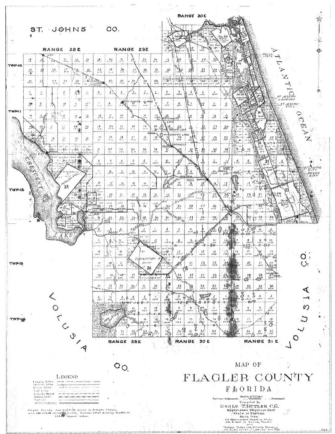

The large map shows a cluster of grants along the rich Graham's Swamp.

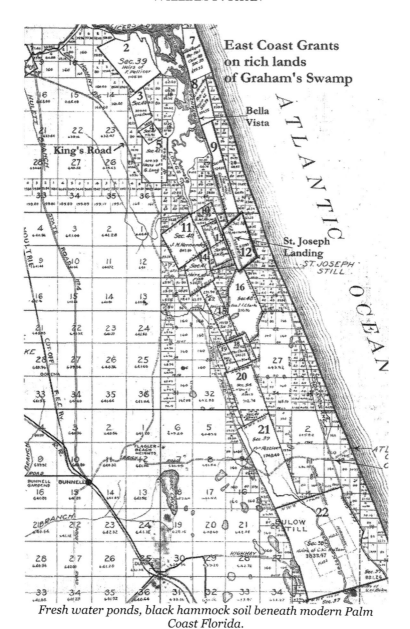

Fresh water ponds, black hammock soil beneath modern Palm Coast Florida.

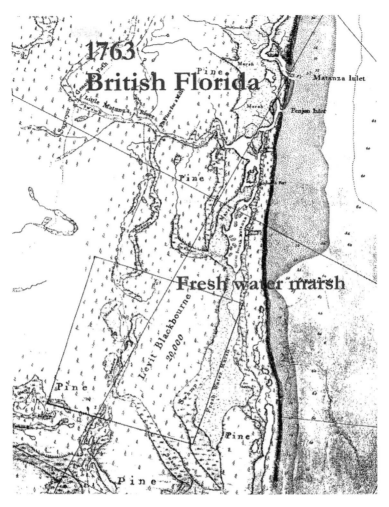

British surveyor deBraum's map of 1763 showed huge tracts of land granted in East Florida to important British officials. Many of these never occupied their property. Levit Blackbourne received 20,000 acres in what later would be called Graham's Swamp. Only a few remaining British land holders could prove their title when the Spanish returned.

18 - Graham's Swamp – John Graham

A 'borrow pit [46] pond along Old King's Road is also at head waters of Bulow Creek and perhaps the location area of one of John Graham's plantations. The Duke stage coach stop was nearby, perhaps west across Old King's.

Located between Old King's road and Colbert lane in modern Palm Coast, Florida are bits of the once great fresh water swamp we call **Graham's Swamp**. It contains the headwaters for Bulow Creek. This great wetland extended from the Matanzas River Lagoon south almost to the Tomoka River and bounded on its east side by scrub and saw palmettos extending to the ocean, and 2-3 miles to the west. In 1823 traveler Charles Vignoles wrote a report on East Florida saying this swamp contained hammock land, which he observed was the most productive in Florida. Unlike so much of Florida land that could be burned out by crops, it was capable of many successive years of rich crops of sugar, corn, hemp and others, he wrote. This great fresh water wet land area was unusual since it was located so near to the salty ocean.

Today this great swamp land has been much changed by roads, gated communities and Florida developers. It is only a fraction of its original size.

When England took Florida from the Spanish who had ruled here for almost 200 years, the King offered great tracts of land to important personages. Some their names on the British surveyor's map of 1764 [47] included:

Richard Oswald 20,000 acres
Levitt Blackbourne 20,000 acres
Arthur Jones 3,000
Peter Taylor 10,000
James Penman 10,000
Andrew Turnbull 20,000
John Grayhurst 20,000
John Moultie 6,000
Theo Townsend 10,000
Clotworthy Upton 20,000
Col. William Faucett 20,000
Capt. Samuel Barrington 20,000
Capt. John Jervis 20,000
William Henry Rickets 20,000

"Large plantations would appear with overseers and slaves with fine homes where the owners may live part time." [48]

The name of Colonel John Graham would not be listed until the very end of the British period and the American Revolution. He would have an effect on the area later to be called by his name.

For 20 years of British rule he was superintendant of Indian affairs in the Western division of the southern district of Florida. In April of 1767 Graham purchased the 500 cattle that would be driven south in a great herd to feed the anticipated arrival of Minorcan settlers in what would become the New Smyrna colony. He paid 27 shillings six pence per head with a plan for 350 of the cattle to go to Mr. Turnbull's arriving settlers, and the balance to Mr. James Penman a local planter in the area. He had correspondence with Dr. Turnbull who had originated the scheme to bring indentured workers from the Island of Minorca in the Mediterranean. Another letter of February 1767 to Dr. Andrew Turnbull describes this cattle purchase to be driven to New Smyrna. [49]

This drive was done in part by an Indian called Grey Eyes who was later credited by British Governor Grant for his aid in locating the path for the King's road through the swamp area south of today's Pellicer Creek. At the end of the American Revolution, many British officers and those loyal to the King were taking refuge in St. Augustine. In December of 1782, John Graham wrote a letter to his superior General Leslie asking for a leave of absence and stating health problems after 30 years service in the Southern Provinces. He had been in St. Augustine and had written that he hoped to return when his health improved. He was observed to be one of the richest loyalists to flee Georgia.

Sometime after that letter of 1782 "Col. John Graham departed Georgia with his two hundred slaves and his four sons. He travelled the King's Road to what was then known as the Levitt Blackbourne Grant of 20,000 acres." [50]

In February 1783 Gov. Tonyn in St. Augustine received a letter from the British government informing him that all Florida residents must be told of the peace treaty that would give Florida to Spain. They were advised to settle their affairs within 18 months. There were delays but the Spanish governor would arrive in June of 1784. Tonyn had issued invitations to the British Royalists in April of 1783 to take their property from the provinces in rebellion and settle in Florida under his protection. Since John Graham arrived here in 1782 he certainly saw the direction in which the revolution was going.

John Graham obtained properties for himself, his brother James Graham, and James' son Joseph Graham. It appears that five tracts or properties were involved. We do not know exactly where they were but Lt. Gov. John Moultrie wrote they were **"3 or 4 miles from a branch of the Matanza (sp) River navigable for Boats and about 32** miles from St. Augustine." [51]

Graham later claimed to the British government that he did *"remove into that Province with upwards of two hundred Negroe(sp) Slaves .....and that at a very heavy expense settled Three different Plantations, Erected Buildings & cleared and planted a considerable quantity of land on each in full confidence of enjoying the fruit of the labor of his Negroes..."* [52]

In his claim to the British government, he did describe some of the activity on the sites.

Lt. Col. John Douglas testified he managed the five Graham family sites that made up his plantations.

"He had 102 men, 67 women and 56 children under his care. That 120 acres were cleared for planting in No. 1 & 2 the two Northernmost tracts and by 1 May 1783 was a large reserve dam begun in November 1782 & they had ditched & dammed part for a rice plantation."

"Upon No 2 there were several buildings raised by the claimant's own Negroes a framed House 30 feet by 18 with cedar planks one story high covered with shingles; a barn 40 feet by 20 framed and covered in the same manner. a kitchen & houses for about 60 working Negroes besides children, they were begun in November 1782 but not finished till June or July 1783..." [53]

"..on No 3 & 4 the two next tracts there were 40 Negroes employed and they had cleared 90 acres before May 1783 & several ditches & drains were begun before April 1783 & worked upon during the whole of that year but never completed. On No 4 there was a log house for an overseer a very good framed barn 30 feet by 18 & Negro houses worth £40. Twenty of these acres were planted with Indigo & 70 with provisions. That in the Summer of 1783 there were 12 acres more cleared upon No.4 which were planted with rice in 1784.."

"..upon No.5 there were 175 acres of swamp land, 50 of Savannah and 275 of pine land..."

"There was an overseer's house, a barn 24 feet by 16 & Negro houses worth about £20." At the end of 1783 Col.

Duncan received a Graham letter saying the Negroes could go to Jamaica in case the province was given up. He said he continued with the improvements not believing the Province would be ceded.

John Graham had located to England and claimed losses of £3,542 and was awarded a payment of £1,011. His lands were abandoned and would later be re-granted to others by the Spanish, most likely becoming the stretch of impressive plantations that extended from Matanzas Inlet down to the Tomoka River.

The area was henceforth called "Graham's Swamp."

It would be nice to believe that a beautiful area with a fresh water lake south of Palm Coast Parkway on Old King's Road in the city of Palm Coast Florida might have been the location for one of Graham's efforts in that it is located so near to Old King's, would be the Duke stage coach stop and has the possibility of water navigation south on the creek which would later to be named for Bulow.

Blooming white water lilies cover this borrow-pit lake, which might be the site of a "lost plantation." The exact Graham locations are lost in the mists of history. This fresh water pond along the Old King's Road could carry some of the answers under its coverage of white flowers. The same Palm Coast historical resources report also mentioned finding "coquina ruins" near the head waters of Smith (later called Bulow) creek, but could not identify them. Perhaps they were part of the lost Graham plantation?

During the second Spanish period, additional grants were made along these swamp hammocks. A few area names were Clarke, McDonnell, Dupont, Fish, Mills, Long, Williams and lastly the John Russell exchange in 1812. Many of these would become "plantations" but history does not record what they did, or of their construction.

These enterprises are long vanished, with perhaps only a brick or fallen chimney lying concealed in the Florida scrub. The winding King's Road that followed ancient Indian trails along raised coquina ridges is being shifted into four lanes, made straight and re-located. The times of the British and

Spanish kings are far behind us. [54]

Surveyor and explorer Charles Vignoles wrote about this area:

"To the south of St. Augustine, there is some very good land on the Matanzas River, which, though having in some places, the poor appearances of beach sand, yet produces cotton of the finest quality, equaling in firmness, and length of staple, the best sea-islands and surpassing the latter in silkiness and texture, so that it commanded five cents more per pound than the cotton of St. Simons in the markets of Liverpool." [55]

19 - Listing of Spanish Grants in Flagler County

Land grants were sold, mortgaged and appear under various names. Here is a **partial list** of Spanish grants in the area of Flagler County Florida: [56] (numbering is from Palm Coast Cultural Assessment report)

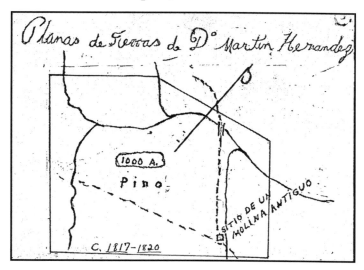

1. **Martin Hernandez**, Sec. 47, 1,003.62 acres (the father of Gen. Joseph Hernandez and site of Hewitt Mill) Pellicer Creek runs through grant as does King's Road. "Site of an old mill" is reference to the Hewitt British colonial era saw mill.

2. **Francis Pellicer** heirs, Sec. 39, 1,104.48 acres (site of Princess Place Preserve near Old King's Road)

3. **C. & G. Clarke**, Sec. 40, 305 acres

4. **M. Mills**, Sec. 41, 113.91 acres

5. **G. Long** heirs, Sec 42, 470.39 acres (later Eatman 1873)

6. **G.W. Perpall**, Sec. 37, 101 acres

7. **G.W. Perpall**, Sec. 38, 599.33 acres Aug 25, 1828 sold 700 acres to Abraham Dupont as Buena Verio. [57] (Dupont also founded town of Matanzas 1829)

8. **J. M. Hernandez**, Sec. 39, 394.75 acres (Bella Vista – Washington Oaks park.)

9. **J. M. Hernandez**, Sec. 40, 724.02 acres (Mala Compra at Bing's Landing.) – site of an archeological dig.

10. **G.W. Perpall**, Sec. 39, 471.42 acres

11. **J.M. Hernandez**, Sec. 40, 807.5 acres Note this grant extends north to the "Long's Creek Landing" which was a historic water shipment point for St. Joseph's Plantation. (Hernandez Landing)

12. **J.M. Hernandez**, Sec. 38, 637.89 acres St. Joseph's, Ruins of this great Sugar Works were destroyed during the construction of modern Palm Coast.

13. **V. Fitzpatrick**, Sec. 43 and 44, 397.07 acres

14. **J. Fish** heirs, Sec. 41, 494.25 acres (later Col. James Williams, New Hartford)

15. **J. Clarke**, Sec. 42, 291.9 acres

16. **George J.F. Clarke**, Sec. 48, 910.56 acres

17. **George J.F. Clarke**, Sec. 50, 199.58 acres

18. **Charles Clarke**, Sec. 51 and 53, 350.97 acres

19. **McDowell and Black**, Sec. 51 and 52, 449.75 acres

20. **McDowell** and Black, Sec. 54 and 40, 903.84 acres

21. **Francis Pellicer**, Sec. 39, 1,745.45 acres (North of Bulow)

22. **C.W. Bulow** heirs, Sec. 38, 3,833.47 acres (Bulowville)

(The following listings were not included in the Palm Coast Cultural Resource Assessment report and were Grants in Western Flagler) Since they were not part of the planned Palm Coast developer, they were likely not included in the report. I found the original grants on the Florida Memories website listed under "Spanish grants." It appears that these were given for service to the Spanish King during the "rebellion" which happened in the "Patriot War" when the new United States was attempting to seize Florida.

23 **Santos Rodriguez**, *Sec. 45 2,622.25 acres*
24. **G.I.F. Clark,** *Sec 40, 296.07 acres*
25. **John Oliveros**, *Sec. 42, 677.42 acres*
26. **F.P. Sanchez**, *Sec. 37 & 37 1,043.46 + 595.92 acres*
27. **Clark & Atkinson** *Sec. 37, 2910.25 acres – Middle Haw Creek*
28. **Anna Madgigine Kingsley** *Sec. 38 & 43) 99.10 acres & 0.9 acres.*

SEARCH FOR THE LOST PLANTATIONS OF FLAGLER COUNTY

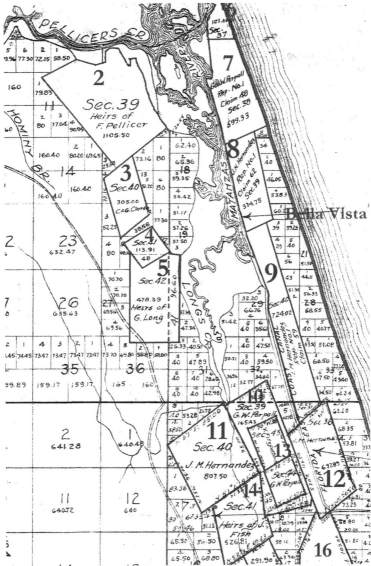

Section of Goold T. Butler C.E. survey map Aug 1926 Flagler County Historical Soc. Grants are marked by author, using those of the Palm Coast Cultural Resource list

There appears to be 27 Spanish land grants in the general Flagler County area. The story of these enterprises was mostly forgotten during the development of Florida. To hold a grant from the King of Spain one was required to prove the property was in usage. This usually involved slaves and agriculture but not always.

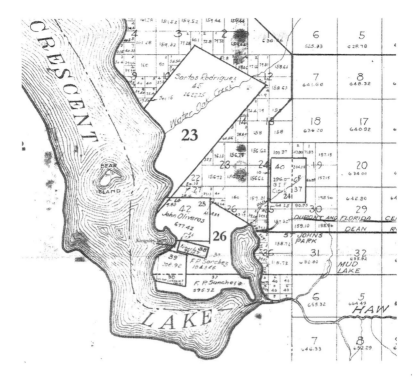

Western Flagler County

Very large grants of land were given adjacent to the water transport potential of "Dunn's Lake" now called Crescent.

St. John's Park and the Bull Creek fish camp are now opposite these great spaces which adjoin to what is presently called "Dead Lake" the last stop of a 1800's steam boat transport line.

Thomas Clarke had obtained extensive amounts of Florida land from the British Governor prior to the second Spanish period. His widow Honoria Clarke divided his claims among her sons James, Charles and George. James settled some 300 acres of an area called by the British as "Worcester" in 1788 and these claims were then some of the first granted by Spain to foreigners in Florida. Brother George established a cattle ranch in 1788 and the three brothers were able to verify their British claims with the Spanish for a total of 1,815.96 acres. While most British had abandoned their lands when Spain took over some remained, pledged allegiance to the Spanish King and remained on their land to establish clear title when the Americans took over in 1821. (3 − sec 40 305 acres)

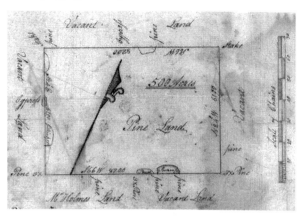

(Wording of a British grant)

Persuant to a warrant from his excellency Patrick Tonyn Esq Governor and Commander in Chief etc. Dated this 3 day of February 1780 Directed to Frederick George Mulcaster Esq. Surveyer General, I have admeasued and laid out to Mrs Honoria Clark a plantation or tract of land measuring 500 acres suituate about sixteen miles south of St. Augustine bounding partialy on lands of John Holmes Esq. and partly on vacent land.....(from grant document)

Since most of the British residents had to depart and try to sell their lands when the Spanish arrived` in 1783 the bulk of the land grants in what would later become Flagler County would be from the Spanish King. Brother George Clarke remained and became and important personage under Spain named as "**Captain of the Northern District of East Florida and Surveyor General of the Provence.**"

Maria Mills was widow of William Mills who obtained

150 acres (4 - Sec. 41) south of a Clarke grant. It was given by Spanish governor White in 1798, and verified by Governor Coppinger in 1819 and confirmed by U.S. authorities in 1827. Her grant referred to nearby "**Johnson's Creek**" which was later called "**Long's Creek.**" This property was upon the Long Grant (5 - section 42 478.39 acres).

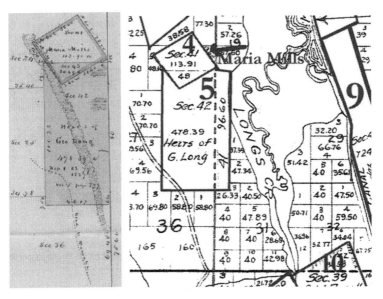

George Long obtained a grant of land adjacent to the winding creek that would bear his name in 1803 from the Spanish governor. He would farm the property for 25 years when it was confirmed by the US authorities in May of 1830. His son Joseph was killed in an Indian attack May 7 1836, while he was trying to warn Mr. Dupont on a nearby plantation. The King's Road ran through the southwestern piece of the grant, and his grant documents mention a "landing" along the creek that would later bear his name. (also called Hernandez Landing) Since Long's Creek would extend north into the Matanzas River, it presented a means of transport of goods via water to oceangoing ships where the Matanzas reached the ocean. (5 – Sec. 42) The property was sold in 1873 to Calvin Eatman.

Gabriel W. Perpall (7 - sec 38) was an important St. Augustine official during the Second Spanish period and was named to be the first mayor of St. Augustine when the Americans took over. He owned much land in Florida some awarded by grant and some purchased. According to the ***Palm Coast Cultural Resource Assessment*** report of 1978, he owned some 1,171 acres of prime land within Flagler County. Abraham Dupont reportedly purchased land from the Perpall eastern grant. [58] He established his home and a plantation here.

Following the acquiring of Florida in 1821 government and local officials began to enact severe laws aimed at the "free black" occupants of the new territory and also directed at recovering what they believed to be escaped slaves. One such law said that all free Negroes living in St. Augustine had to have a white guardian or owner which would force those even having small businesses to seek out such a person. Gabriel W. Perpall was listed as a guardian for several families placed in this position.

20 - The Pellicer Plantation

Princess Place Preserve is today a beautiful Flagler County park near Old King's road in the northern part of the county. It was once part of a hunting lodge complex of Mr. Henry Cutting in 1866 when the area was called Cherokee Grove.

Long before this time in 1788, **Francisco Pellicer** received a Spanish land grant for 1,105 acres at the confluence of Matanzas River and Pellicer Creek, built a house where 12 of his 18 children were born. (2 – 39 1105.50 acres)

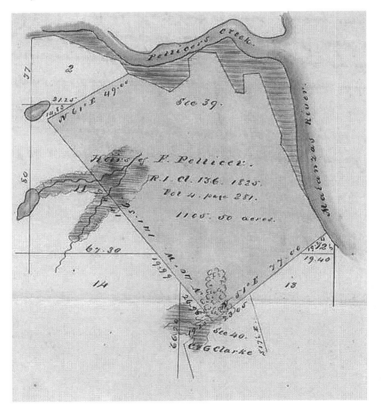

There's no location established for his house in the county park, but it should rate as "a plantation". He died in 1820. In an application for another grant in 1818, he said his present location was 'irrigable land and pine forest, all not useful." Further, he had lost his livestock to Indian raids.

In 1802 Pellicer's home may have been fortified against attacks. The nearby waterway was named for him as Pellicer Creek. There is some indication his home also was burned in an attack. Mr. Pellicer and his family were fortunately in St. Augustine while his house at Pellicer creek was destroyed and a servant called Jenny was taken away by the Indians.

Donald F. Pellicer, a fifth generation descendent said the Spanish land grant to his ancestor and the modern park limits were the same. A hint to the location of the Pellicer home lies in a very old map drawn in 1838.

I could not locate a study to give the location of his home but I do believe the map drawn by a Col. Fanning and Maj. Ashby (1838) during the Seminole War might give a hint.

This map shows the "Twin Bridges" of King's road as it crossed Pellicer Creek. To the south and east the road on this map are shown as "Cultivated Land with a little circle that may have indicated a house site. Historians at the Princess Place preserve have never located the Pellicer house.

This information first appeared in my book *"The Search for Old King's Road."* Computer enhancement of the old map seems to indicate the location for a house. "Cultivated Land" was likely on the Pellicer Plantation. Enlarged section of Pellicer Creek area with the King's Road that may show location of Pellicer property on a Spanish land grant.

This greatly enlarged area of a soldiers "sketch map" shows the "twin bridges" across the Pellicer Creek and Hewett Branch creeks with what may be the site of the Pellicer home located to the right and next to what appears to be part of the Pellicer plantation marked as cultivated land. These are crude drawings from a soldier's record book and may not have accurate scale. Hewitt's old mill is shown in this map.

21 - Jesse Fish Deserves a Full Book

Just south of Hernandez St. Joseph Plantation are some 526.81 acres granted to Jesse Fish. (14 - sec 41) It was later to be called "New Hartford." This planter lived through incredible adventures being a merchant, a trader of slaves, a real estate agent perhaps a spy, and certainly a smuggler. His family was seafaring merchants and as a young boy he arrived in St. Augustine during the first Spanish period. He lived with an important Spanish family who treated him as their son.

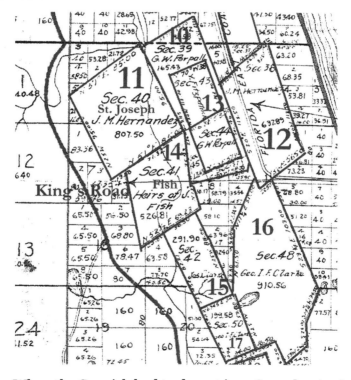

When the Spanish had to depart in 1763 and 1764 there was desperation to sell land to whoever had funds. Fish became a hidden realtor and thus had title to much land. He speculated in great tracts of land. He also was noted for growing oranges, and providing juice to the English market. In the latter part of his life he had business reverses and lost most of his property.

The property, which was known as 'Todd's Fields' was granted by the Spanish Governor on 1 April 1791. Jesse Fish reportedly died on April 1, 1790. Thus his son Jesse Fish Jr. may have inherited this property and was able to verify the grant from Governor Quesada; however, Jesse Fish Jr. died in 1812 when struck by lightning. He did not leave a will so his mixed race wife Clarissa could not inherit. [59] The property was confirmed to the other Fish heirs by the US government in 1825 as 526.81 acres. Their application document said the Plantation had been cultivated by the Fish family from 1 April 1791 to the 1825 submission. [60]

Title was then obtained by Gabriel W. Perpall. James William purchased this property which was listed as an active plantation and he called it 'New Hartford'. He reportedly had 30 slaves on the Plantation plus himself and his wife. New Hartford was destroyed during the Seminole War of 1835 and sold at auction in 1896. [61] I calculate it was an active Plantation for about 45 years from 1791 to 1836 when it was destroyed.

I regret not knowing the entire Fish Jr. story which involves his wife and children described as 'mixed race' and that of wife Clarisa who was owner of a house in St. Augustine with eight other free residents and one slave. [62] Jesse Fish was noted for his shipment of oranges to England. His oranges were used in a popular drink called shrub and were prized as being the very best in sweetness. Could it be that some of these excellent orange products were shipped out of "Hernandez Landing" to become a popular drink in England? When Fish died most of his extensive investments had been lost and his large plantation on Anastasia Island fallen into disrepair.

WILLIAM P. RYAN

An area west of "Dead Lake" [63] and present day St. John's Park in western Flagler appears to have been designated for rewards to those who aided the Spanish cause. They were located along 'Dunn's Lake' which is present day Crescent Lake.

22 - In Reward for Services to the King

On March 13, 1812, a group of volunteers, mostly from Georgia, invaded Florida and aided by some U.S. gunboats seized the port of Fernandina. This began the "Patriot War" against Spanish occupied Florida. The objective was to seize the rich lands of Florida which they believed were poorly held by a weak Spanish government.

There was much confusion as to who was loyal to the Spanish and who would fight for the intruders. The Spanish enlisted free Negro allies and repelled the invaders, who also were now repudiated by the U.S. government in the person of James Monroe who was then Secretary of State.

From this wild and uncertain time, just prior to the War of 1812, many Spanish land grants were issued in reward for loyal services given to Spain during the Patriot actions.

If you stand at the present Bull Creek fish camp, located in Western Flagler County, you can look across "Dead Lake" to view great stands of dense woodlands. Here once were immense plantations and land grants that are long forgotten.

"Dead Lake" was the last steam boat stop, and is far from dead. It connects to Crescent Lake (Dunn's Lake) and the St. John's River, once an important ship connection

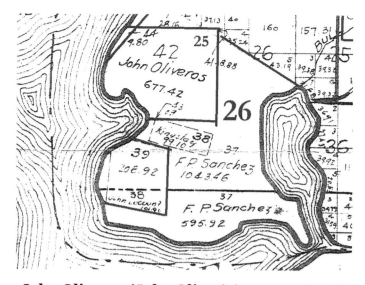

John Oliveros (John Oliver) (25 – sec 42) applied to the U.S. government for title on his large 677.42 acre property saying he farmed it from 1818 to 1822. His title application gives a hint of his "plantation" when he wrote:"..*two years prior to the exchange of flags and that after he got his buildings up he was taken sick and continued so for nearly twelve months without being able to work. That since the exchange of flags he made several improvements in the land that has fields planted of about twenty five acres with corn and rice, and some sugar cane, and has eight or nine Negroes on the plantation...*" [64] Oliver or Oliveras said in his claim he had received no grants from either the Spanish or the British but had occupied the land for two years prior to the U.S. taking over Florida. None of his documents tells how he obtained the land. However, his application does bear the word "**donation**." It is not known which side of the Patriot issue held Mr. Oliver. His claim covers the 1821 date when the U.S. took over Florida. It was first refused in 1824 and then was apparently accepted by the U.S. Commission in 1825 although the Florida Memories documents fail to present copies of an original Spanish Land grant as did so many other applicants.

Anna Madgigine Kingsley (28 – sec. 38) was the African wife of Zephaniah Kingsley. Both were very much involved in the Patriot action. She is listed as the owner of a small grant below that of Mr. Olivares. Her application to the U.S. Government to confirm Spanish grants of land tells a story that differs a bit from other published ones:

Application for confirmation of 350 acres St. Augustine 19 December 1815 -

"Anna Madgigine Kingsley, a free Negro and inhabitant of the River St. John in this province with the respect due to your Excellency states that on 13 September 1813, the Governor, your Excellency's predecessor thought it to grant her five acres of land at a spot situated between those occupied by Don Juan Creighton and Don Enrique Wrights for the reason set forth in the proceeding annexed, and for the purpose therein mentioned. that in effect she built her principal house and some smaller ones for six slaves which she possesses with all other things necessary and considered herself safe from the insults and annoyances of the insurgents. But towards the end of the year, a party of Bandits from Georgia under the command of a captain named Alexander having approached from Georgia with a design of robbing the peaceable inhabitants, the gunboats which from the River were on the lookout for the coming of the enemy observed that many land buildings might serve as a shelter and protection to them, and for this reason the commandant ordered (bf by author) the new establishment to be destroyed and burnt as it was done with what it contained, the flames destroying much corn and other things amounting to the value of more than fifteen hundred dollars because the best service of his Majesty required it. In virtue thereof and that your memoralist has an increased family of three children, six slaves and 20 head of cattle which from having no lands of her own the keeper of those of Don Zephaniah Kingsley she therefore prays your Excellency to be pleased to extend for her said compensation with a right of possession until she acquires the legal title by performing the conditions prescribed for that purpose to three hundred and fifty acres

which she thinks compensated to her and her......end of document record. [65]

This application was written apparently from the Spanish point of view as historians later wrote that Anna Kingsley had decided to burn her own plantation in order to keep the raiders from benefiting from it. Her husband Zephaniah Kingsley was also held hostage by the rebels who claimed he was a supporter.

Anna had established her own plantation. As a free black female under Spanish rules she could own property and have slaves under her control. She thus had established her own place.

The piece of land in Western Flagler County marked as section 38 for 99.10 acres was apparently part of a larger grant given to her and acknowledged by the U.S. Commissioners on 1825. Author Daniel L. Schafer in his book ***Anna Madgigine Jai Kingsley*** published in 2003 noted that this piece may not have been occupied by Anna, and was possibly sold later for unpaid taxes.

John Lecount (38 & 39) produced a survey map copy dated 26 April 1821, when the U.S. was taking over Florida. His map was said to be a duplicate of an original survey done by Don George Clarke, Surveyor General for Spanish Florida on August 11, 1815 after Lecount was granted 300 Acres of land next to Dunn's Lake. His request stated he was an inhabitant of Fernandina (where the Patriot troubles began) and that he "served the government at the period of the revolution without pay and rations." While documents generated near the U.S. take over of Florida were viewed by the U.S. Commission with suspicion, Lecount was given title to the property.

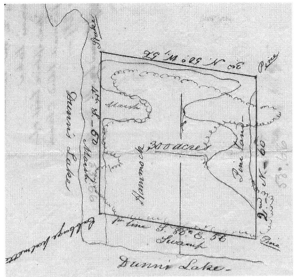
John Lecount grant section 38 & 39

Francis P. Sanchez (26 – sec 37) appears to have purchased a Spanish grant from a Fernando de la Mara Arredondo who was awarded some 2,700 acres of land in April 1806 for services to the Spanish during the rebellion. The property was sold on December 15, 1817. The documents indicate that land was awarded by Don Jose Coppinger to *"officers and soldiers both of the line, as well as militia and other individuals of this province who contributed to its defense at the time of the Rebellion being one of said rewards the distribution of lands."*

This was an immense piece of land located adjacent to Dunn's Lake (Crescent Lake) with good transport potential to connections on the St. John's River.

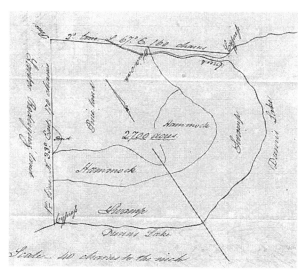

This survey is one of the multitudes done by George Clarke who was the Surveyor General for the Spanish government and who kept all of the records. Others on Dunn's Lake were not approved by the U.S. Commission including McDowall & Black, Charles Gobert, and John Ashton all of whom appeared to be related to the rebellion indicating this land "Donation" area was established by the Spanish government.

Santos Rodriguez (23-45) was an attorney under the Spanish second rule in Florida and had title to an immense property of some 2,622.25 acres of land along the north western shore of Dunn's Lake (Crescent Lake). A stream called Water Oak Creek flowed through the property. Again with contact to the immense lake and St. John's River, his property would be ideal as a plantation. The Spanish land grant documents dated 1818 indicate that this too was awarded for service during the "Rebellion."

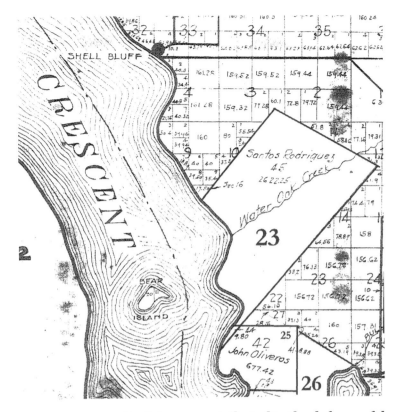

"Don Santos Rodriguez contributed to the defense of the province in time of the rebellion" Spanish land grant document dated 1818. [66]

Martin Hernandez (1- sec. 47) Spanish land grant, part of a 2,000 acre reward given by Gov. Coppinger also for military service to Martin Hernandez, father of Gen. Joseph Hernandez on September 16, 1817. Located in north Flagler along Pellicer Creek, this paper shows the old sawmill site of Hewitt (probably destroyed around 1812.)

Sketch of Martin Hernandez grant shows site of "Old Mill." Old sketch map clearly shows the bridge across Pellicer Creek, the King's Road, and the Spring Garden trail to Volusia. Pellicer is called "Northwest Creek" on this rendering. The area was very swampy with the British-built raised causeway for the King's Road likely still existing south of the bridge and leading to the ruins of the old sawmill.

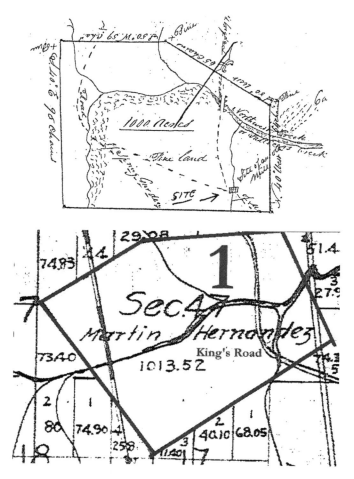

23 - The Spanish Surveyor

George J.F. Clarke (Clark) and his brothers held an amazing amount of land claims in Florida likely derived from his position as the official surveyor for the Spanish government. He most certainly was awarded lands for his services.

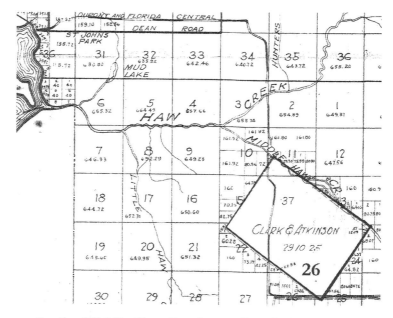

On the Middle Haw Creek was the Clark and Atkinson land of 2,910.25 acres. George Atkinson had claims for 15,000 acres rejected by the U.S. Commission including this claim for 3,000 acres in 1828. It apparently was then approved by a combined claim with Clark (26 – sec. 37). This area is close to the present Flagler "Cody's Corners."

I could not discover what activity took place on these Clark lands but it would be logical that they were in usage and I have listed them as "Plantations." Since the surveyor Clarke held all the Spanish records at one time, his claims would have great effect on the U.S. Commission set up to prove ownership in the new Florida when it became part of the United States after the Spanish departed in 1821.

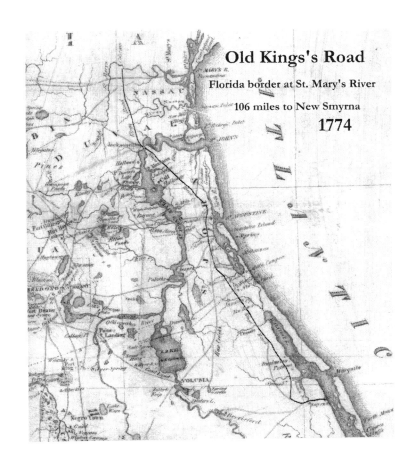

24 - We Must Have a Good Road

When the British arrived in 1763, they needed settlers. To encourage travel into Florida the King's Road was completed around 1774 prior to the American Revolution

The King's Road to the north would connect to a good path that led to Savannah, Georgia. It crossed the St. Mary's river at the Florida and Georgia border, continued south to "Cow Ford" which is today's Jacksonville, then to St. Augustine. Arriving in what would be today's Flagler County Florida, it passed by Hewitt's sawmill after crossing the Pellicer Creek at the site called "Twin Bridges." Engineers built raised causeways across the swamps to offer a smooth, carriage and wagon ready roadway that led south to the high bluffs of the Tomoka River (later called Buckhead's Bluff) then further south to New Smyrna.

Measuring sixteen feet across, with ditches and pine logs laid crosswise in the wet portions and causeways through the swamps and bridges across the many creeks and rivers, the commodious King's Road beckoned to migrants from the northern colonies Regular stagecoach travel was begun.

The British occupation of Florida might be called its

"first land development." When the British Governor James Grant arrived in 1764, he made establishment of roads into Florida his priority. He knew that to bring in settlers he needed a suitable roadway vital to populate the wild spaces of Florida. British surveyor Gerard deBrahm began his surveys and produced the first accurate maps of Florida. He laid out possible routes for this new road.

By 1774, a complete, well-made highway was finished and was called The King's Road. It extended from the northern St Mary's River (now the Florida northern border) down to the new colony of New Smyrna. The roadway then connected to existing routes leading north to Savannah. This remarkable road of 106 miles remained a main entryway into Florida and was in usage as long as 1914. [67] It was often paved with the crushed white shell from the ancient Indian mounds. Hard working slaves using primitive hand tools had accomplished what would later be called '**The most important Civil Engineering project in America.**' [68]

Several rich plantations had existed near the King's Road. One of the early ones was that of Richard Oswald. He was granted 20,000 acres in 1766. [69] Here the once thriving Timucuan village of Nocoroco once stood. Mount Oswald was managed by an agent for Oswald who remained in England. "It was the lush acres along the Halifax and Tomoka Rivers, which extended from what today is Tomoka State Park, Ormond Beach, to present day Holly Hill, that were developed by Oswald into thriving plantations. "On Mount Oswald Plantation there was a 40 x 20' dwelling house, a large barn, stable, kitchen, overseer's house, corn house and other outhouses. Four miles south of Mount Oswald, on the Tomoka River was the Ferry Settlement, on which were a hundred acres of high land cleared for corn and rice. There was also a ferry there crossing the Tomoka River, a ferry house, and a smith's shop. A few miles south of Ferry Settlement was Oswald's Cowpen Settlement, which was a small clearing, made for raising cattle. Oswald's Adia Settlement was located on the Halifax River, and contained an overseer's house, indigo house, and huts for the slaves, and a hundred acres of land cleared for indigo and corn." 70

"The British offered some 144 land grants in Florida after first invalidating any property claims from the first Spanish period. Some early British grants were John Grayhurst on East side of Crescent Lake, Lewis Blackbourne south of the Matanzas river headwaters and within what would later be called Graham's swamp, and the Townsend tract at the southwest corner of the county." 71 The planters offered naval stores of tar, pitch, turpentine and resin plus rice, indigo, cattle, timber and citrus.

When the British were forced to depart following the American Revolution, their fine plantations fell into ruin. The Spanish faced with the same problem of repopulating Florida, begin to issue Land Grants to new settlers. Unfortunately, some of those obtaining land were of doubtful loyalty to the then weak Spanish government.

What would later become the Bulow Plantation was about 4-5 miles north of Oswald's.

During the British era, plantations were established which included the settlement of Dr. Andrew Turnbull at New Smyrna. In 1767, he transported some 1,403 settlers in eight ships from Greece, Minorca and Italy. He had planned for Indentured Labor with a promise of land after his workers spent a certain time in his colony. His plans did not succeed and many died or suffered. They escaped by going up the King's Road to St. Augustine. Thousands of loyalists had fled the American colonies during the American Revolution and settled in St. Augustine. "The population of East Florida, normally around 3,000 persons, had rapidly swelled with the arrival of 5,000 British Loyalists and 8,000 slaves during the years 1778 to 1782." 72 In their 20 years of occupation the British had built a fine road and expended considerable investment in large plantations and settlements.

In June 1783 the British discover they must depart.

Spain was an ally of the new American nation. Bernardo de Galvez had captured West Florida during the American Revolution. During the intense negotiation to settle this war in Paris, it was said that Benjamin Franklin swapped England right out of Florida. This was terrible news to the British planters who had invested large sums in Florida's development. St. Augustine was again to be almost deserted except for the new Minorcan refugee groups that were of the Catholic faith and would have good future relationships with the incoming Spanish plus the few settlers who wished to remain with the Spanish.

In June 1784 Spanish Governor Vicente Manuel de Zespedes arrived. Spain faced many problems. Wars in Europe, sifting alliances, and invasions prevented proper funding and support of their new colony of Florida. Land hungry settlers from the new United States were settling along the St. Mary's River border. Some would be loyal to Spain but most would not. [73] The Seminole Indians and other groups that were forced into Florida by war were resisting the many slave hunters that now invaded Florida seeking what they called 'run away' slaves.

In 1807 England had abolished slavery in its domains. The demand for labor in Georgia, the Carolinas and the American south resulted in much raiding into Florida by slavers. In 1807 and 1808, slave trade had also been abolished by the Spanish. Slaves in Spanish Florida had retained the right to own property, testify in court, have relief from an abusive master, and even financial negotiation for their liberty. These rights did not exist to the north in the new United States.

In 1790 under great pressure, Spanish authorities cancelled their policy of protecting escaped slaves. Spain held on in Florida for some 38 years until July 1821 when the Spanish flag was lowered. When Thomas Jefferson was US President he issued his Non Intercourse Act forbidding Americans from trading with Europe. The theory was to be separated from the European wars. U.S. ships either rotted in harbor or could not return home. As a result, in 1807 the Spanish port of Fernandina became an active smugglers' area much to the dismay of the American authorities. As many as 150 ships of various nations could be viewed in the harbor. [74] In March of 1812 a group calling themselves The Patriots were secretly supported by the US government as they invaded Florida including Fernandina.

A Revolutionary War officer, 72 year old, George Matthews was placed in command. The Americans were enraged when the Spanish fielded armed black soldiers from St. Augustine. The raids by the Patriots were repulsed and later repudiated officially by the President James Madison. The Patriots did cause much damage in Florida. Spain became weaker with changes in its government, and was unable to pay their Florida soldiers. The US also had made claims for some American ships captured by privateers and said Spain owned them 5 million dollars for these and other possible claims by US citizens including perhaps escaped slaves. In 1819, the United States obtained title to all of Florida in settlement of this very doubtful "debt" they said the Spanish owed.

Florida was then a wild place with pirates, freebooters, land seekers, and slave hunters roaming and bothering its residents. Although the Spanish government gave large numbers of land grants to encourage settlement it was not a peaceful time. It took courage and much hope for someone to invest their money and begin life in Spanish Florida. Those that took the Spanish land grants were brave men with holding optimism for the future. They invested their lives, their families and their money in the future of Florida and their hopes for profit and a good life. The excellent King's Road had deteriorated due to lack of maintenance and almost vanished south of the Tomoka River.

25 - A Plantation for Trees – Hewitt's Mill

Lumbermen cut live oak near the Hewitt Mill site. The giant trees are gone.

Early Florida had many huge trees. The long leaf pine (now almost extinct), the ancient live oak hundreds of years old all grew to immense size The wood was a treasure both for ship building and the early settlers. Prior to the American Revolution Mr. John Hewitt acquired a British grant for 1,000 acres of land near Pellicer Creek and began his water-powered mill in the midst of great stands of valuable, ancient trees. By 1770, he was supplying lumber to the British colony of northeast Florida.

Following the revolution St. Augustine was packed with loyalist refugees desperate for housing. New arrivals were estimated at 17,375 of escaping loyalists and their slaves. [75] The Hewitt mill cut lumber for construction in St. Augustine. It was an industrial complex containing overseer's house, sawyer's house, slave houses, kitchens, carpenter and blacksmith's shops, fields for grain plus housing for oxen and animals. [76]

Captain Robert Bisset had been hired to construct a section of the King's road south from Pellicer Creek and took it past the sophisticated hydraulic mill of Hewitt much improving the ability to ship lumber to St. Augustine. [77]

Unlike the millraces in northern states, Florida rarely has running water. Thus using slave labor with primitive tools and oxen large collection areas were dug along what is called "Hewitt Branch" a stream that leads north to the slow flowing Pellicer Creek. A dam was constructed across this swampy area to store and maintain the water height needed to power a mill wheel. This created a large area of water stored to the south of these dams where water could be used as a millpond. Gates and spillway were used to regulate the water height. Much earth had to be moved and relocated possibly with oxen pulled scoops. This complex and very sophisticated system stored power for the mill. A small diameter broad undershot wheel known as a flutter wheel provided power from the water that then flowed into a discharge pond.

The mill had an automatic feed system via a complex system of levers. The cutting saw ran up and down in vertical motion. Movements within the mill were regulated by directing the flow of water. This 'hydraulic' mill was highly sophisticated technology of its time.

The mill was likely in operation up to the "Patriot War" times of 1812 when it may have been abandoned and burned. Articles located at the site show signs of deliberate destruction and fire. [78]

Archaeologist Dana Ste. Claire wrote: **"This is the only known Revolutionary War period dam and sawmill in the state of Florida. It is not only one of a kind. It is incredibly well preserved and just a truly magnificent site."**

Researcher William M. Jones spent much time at the site writing reports and collecting artifacts. His work documented much of this historic site.

In 2007, Palm Coast Holdings turned the 10-acre site over to the nearby Florida Agricultural Museum and donated some $350,000 for signage and access bridges to the historic site. However except for guided tour group access to the site it was difficult to visit due to the lack of a good turn off from US 1 highway. The site was hard to reach. Engineers from the St. Johns Water Management district had also helped to locate the King's Road from the site north to the causeway built by the British across the swamp area south of Pellicer Creek. The fields of white water Lilly and tall Cypress trees can now be viewed by only a few who were fortunate to walk on the raised causeway of this old British road that still exists here.

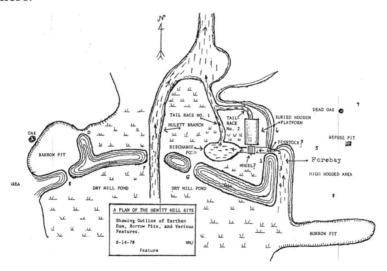

A detailed wooden model of the mill apparatus was constructed by Mr. Jones and was later presented as part of a Hewitt Mill display at the Florida Agricultural Museum.

The mill and its supporting buildings can be observed as one of Florida's early 'plantations' with the product produced being sawed lumber. The large live oak trees and long leaf pines have vanished due to years of lumbering at the site.

Water still flows thru some of the channels located by Mr. Jones. A brass plaque commemorating this site was placed there on an overlook bridge by the Daughters of the American Revolution. The immense earthworks there are a memory of difficult slave labor in the late 1700's. The mounds of earth that comprise the dams were moved using only simple hand tools and great amounts of labor. I once stood here reflecting this was the most logical spot for water and food for the escaping Minorcan refugees as they journeyed up Old King's Road. Once they crossed Pellicer Creek, they were headed for civilization. This area was also called "Twin Bridges" by the locals. Many historical artifacts were located in 1978 by researcher Jones, but no one could tell me of their present location. The 1978 report of Mr. Jones exists at the Flagler County Historical Society annex.

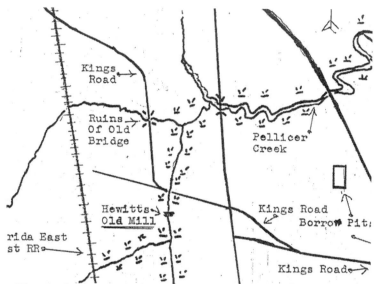

Here is the location of colonial era saw mill and British built King's Road south of Pellicer Creek and adjacent to present US1 in Flagler County Florida. The King's Road ran through the area which included a large wetland and a raised causeway across the swamp area. It was built by the British for a connection to Pellicer Creek. (Map by William M. Jones)

A raised causeway runs through swamp areas south of Pellicer Creek near the Hewitt Mill site. Public access at present is limited as this land is presently within a St. John's Water Management district property. The raised British causeway still exists on an ancient road that runs through this wetland. The causeway is in surprisingly good condition. (causeway photo Bill Ryan)

26 - Fort Fulton February 21, 1840

Near to the Hewitt Mill and also researched by Mr. Jones was a Seminole War era fort located close to present US1. Flagler teacher Mr. Buddy Taylor took classes to the site for "digs" and maintained a small museum of artifacts located at his school. Unfortunately the museum and its relics no longer exist. [79] Several local officials had hoped that the unique Hewitt Mill site and this log fort would be developed for visitation, including the King's Road section that the Fort Fulton would be made accessible. Unfortunately like so much of Florida history these sites are forgotten or tangled in legal issues of land ownership. Many valuable artifacts at the Mill site were also indexed by Mr. Jones but their present location is unknown.

"There was information relative to the presence of Volunteer Militia Troops in the Pellicer Creek area as early as January 1840, or about a month before the time Fulton was said to have been established."

"Can anyone inform us why the mounted Volunteer Company, raised in this city, and now stationed at Hewlett's Mill is weakened by a detail of ten men subject to the order of the City Council and kept in town idle?" Florida Herald, St. Augustine January 17 1840 [80]

Likely site of Fort Fulton visited by William Ryan and Jim Massfeller in 2010. It is upon a small hill with white sugar sand at the mapped location. This is the first known photograph of the location. photo Bill Ryan

Typical log fort of the Seminole War (photo Florida Agricultural Museum). There have been several groups desiring to protect the historic Old King's Road, the Hewitt Mill site and the known site of the Fort Fulton.

"Several excavations appear on the site of Fort Fulton, pointing to the activities of relic collectors. These people have been credited with the removal of military artifacts including a cache of 150 musket shot; a brass butt plate for a firearm; and several military and pewter buttons. These materials, among with others not reported are now scattered about the State and it would be next to impossible to compile an accurate list of these recovered items." [81] Several local historians have spoken of the "wonderful historic potential" consisting of Hewitt's Mill, Old King's road, the British

Causeway, Pellicer Creek and Fort Fulton. These comprise a unique location in Florida.

William Jones (right) excavates Hewitt sawmill timbers in the 1970's and did extensive reporting on the site. Many artifacts were located and a model of the "hydraulic" mill was donated to the Florida Agricultural Museum.

Shipbuilder John Russell

Photo composite image by author

He acquires lands that would become Bulowville
John Russell was born in South Carolina near Charleston in 1766. He became a builder of fine ships but he was caught up in the American Revolution. He remained loyal to the King and in 1783 sailed to the Bahamas with his tools, slaves and family. He was listed as a 'Tory traitor' and had his name placed on the "Traitor's listing" so that his Charleston shipyard could be seized. His new yard was on Hog Island in the Bahamas and he began to make fine ships again. He received several land grants in the Bahamas and expanded his business. His son and a daughter were born in the Bahamas.

His ship building business was ruined by war and the Embargo of Thomas Jefferson. .In 1811 Russell swore allegiance to the King of Spain in St. Augustine. On 1811 he had sailed his finest ship which was a two mast schooner called "Perseverence" across the shallow and difficult St. Augustine entrance. His ship was 54 feet in length, 16 ½ feet in the beam, and drew only six feet of water when loaded. It could carry as much as 300 flour barrels and cross the difficult St. Augustine entry bar. It was reputed to be fast, well built and was fully equipped with sails and cordage. The interior was fine mahogany. He arrived at St. Augustine with his family, 40 slaves, and a Captain called Don Thomas Forrest.

The Spanish governor pro tempore Don Juan Jose de Estrada had problems. His treasury was nearly empty. Most of the food supply for St. Augustine had to be imported. He badly needed a good ship of shallow draft that could enter the St. Augustine harbor.

After many complex negotiations Russell was granted some 4,000 acres plus 675 additional in exchange for his Schooner. The 675 acres extra was given for the size of his family and number of slaves owned. Normally Spanish title was not passed on a land grant until the unit had been farmed for 10 years. Russell believed his well-equipped ship was worth at least $5,000 more than the settlement price. He had slaves and property in Bermuda that he could not bring to Florida due to the war of 1812, nor could he have this new land surveyed.

The Spanish would rename his ship the Barbarita.

Eventually the deal was done, and Russell could occupy a grant of land site on 10 July 1812. [82] He had negotiated for immediate title. He named the property "Good Retreat" which may have some meaning since he was abandoning his shipbuilding and starting a new career as a planter. However he died in July of 1814 in the home of his daughter at Fernandina before final title passed as the land had not been surveyed. His wife Mary and eldest son James had to continue negotiations to obtain clear title. [83]

On June 21, 1821, Francisco Pellicer and others took John Russell's son James H. to the property where he rode about on horseback, broke branches, threw sand in the air and other acts to show ownership. 25 June 1821 Spanish surveyor Clarke wrote a document describing the boundaries for Russell heir land to be sold to Charles Bulow. Location was in a place then called as "Graham's Swamp." No buildings were shown on the survey nor were any mentioned in the documents, so we do not know if Russell was able to build or develop on his property.

A survey was made on 19 July 1821 and listed there were 3,480 acres of land in Grahams Swamp located between Ormond and Francis Pellicer properties. Shown on survey as swamp land and no buildings were noted. (Other records showed 4,675 acres) [84]

In August 1821 the Russell heirs sold a listed 4,675 acres to Charles W. Bulow of Charleston S.C. for $9,944.50 in cash. [85]

It is remarkable that some of the Russell family still live in Flagler County located in what is called the Hammock area!

27 - July 10, 1831 Spanish Flag is Removed

On July 10 1821, the Spanish flag was removed from the Castillo de San Marcos. St. Augustine was again a much-reduced town as many had departed. In addition, a Yellow Fever outbreak was raging perhaps arriving in the Spanish transports from Havana where the disease was rampant. Sometime in April 1821 the Black and Indian town of Angola on the Western side of Florida also were raided by slave hunters possibly connected to Andrew Jackson. Soon after the Spanish departed, a party of desperate Seminole Indians arrived at the St. Augustine gates on July 16th seeking aid from the slavers and Angola raid. [86] The Spanish had sailed and Indian hope for refuge or defense against the slave raiders went with the Spanish. The hunt for 'escaped' slaves now became a business throughout Florida. The young United States held Florida. Land speculators, buyers and slavers flooded in.

Charles W. Bulow arrived in St. Augustine and purchased a town house, which likely would become his base for establishing a new plantation in Florida that would later be called Bulowville or the Bulow Plantation. He purchased the house from Donna Maria de la Conception Miranda on 6 April 1821. It was located on Marine Street on the Bay "by which it is bounded on the East, on the West by the heirs of Antonio Benton and on the West by the house of Martin Hernandez" (Gen. Hernandez father). [87] To see how he arrived here you need to know something of the Bulow family that lived in Charleston South Carolina. There is also some family legends told, a story of Ms. Emily Bulow that is not proven, but if true it would explain much about later events that happened on the Bulow plantation.

Reconstruction of BULOW SUGAR MILL

28 - The Bulow Family of Charleston

In the 1750's (exact date unknown) Joachim Von Bulow arrived in Charleston, South Carolina, from Meckenburg Germany and was listed as a Lutheran Minister. He acquired much property, was married and had two sons and a daughter, Anna Elizabeth. His oldest son John Joachim Bulow was born in 1765 and younger son Charles Wilhelm Bulow was born in 1778.

Charles Wilhelm Bulow – the younger son

In 1783 the father billed the South Carolina legislature for supplies provided the South Carolina forces during the revolution as he supported the rebel cause. It was recorded that he had large warehouses full of food and material that he sold to the South Carolina revolutionary troops. Thus unlike many of his neighbors his property was not seized. [88]

The two brothers were in the cotton business together. The family also had a fine cotton plantation called 'Savannah' and grew in wealth. The elder brother inherited large tracts of land including his "magnificent" plantation. [89]

The younger son Charles Wilhelm was reported to have gained more wealth during the shipping embargo. He had a great house on Meeting Street in Charleston. In 1807 President Jefferson and later President Madison launched a 'Shipping Embargo' from US ports to keep the young United States out of the never-ending European wars.

The Port of Fernandina, then in Spanish Florida, became full of smugglers, retired pirates and those wishing to avoid the term of the Embargo that had idle American ships rotting in US ports. [90] It can be believed that Charles Wilhelm made active connections to move embargoed cotton, and perhaps in exchange for desirable goods from Europe during this period.

The Bulows were said to have made a fortune during the embargo; a euphuism for speculation in cargoes of blockade runners."

A younger son could not inherit the family fortune which would go to Brother John Joachim Bulow, thus younger Charles Wilhelm would wish to grow his own wealth. He was apparently of an adventurous nature. The Bulow family was very wealthy, had access to a fine cotton plantation in Charleston and was successful in the cotton trade. They would have access to the best artisans among their extensive slave holdings.

Under Spanish rule many land grants were being assigned in Florida, but times were wild there during the War of 1812 between the US and England.

In 16 January of 1803 the younger son, Charles Wilhelm Bulow had married Adelaide Fowler Johnston and a son, John Joachim was born around 1807. In March of 1812 "Patriots" were attacking Spanish St. Augustine and the port of Fernandina could no longer be used.

Their son John Joachim Bulow was sent to Paris 'for his education' sometime around 1812. This would make him only 4 to 5 years old. It is possible he never again met his Charleston family until his return upon the death of his father Charles Wilhelm Bulow. Charles Wilhelm died at his town house home in St. Augustine on May of 1823. [91] He is buried in the "Huguenot" Cemetery there. His death was only three short years after arriving in St. Augustine.

Sending the small son in 1812 to France is another mystery. The Bulow family was wealthy and could accomplish almost anything. Napoleon was in France at that time, a U.S. war with England was brewing and Napoleon had begun his famous and disastrous campaign against Russia in 1812.

Why then was John Joachim placed on a ship for Paris while only a young child? Perhaps the Bulows made some contacts with French friends during the Embargo of 1807. Was France a place for their son to be located during these times of war?

Could it have anything to do with his "adopted" older sister Emily? Alternatively, was there fear that Charleston would be attacked as it was during the Revolution?

These are only guesses.

Whatever the reason, this young boy went to Paris for his education and (perhaps) never again met his father.

29. - The Legend of an Indian Princess

*Images from William Lenssen, Palm Coast Florida

There is a family legend concerning Emily Bulow. If true it has been concealed for some 200 years. It would go far to explain why young John Joachim Bulow repeatedly said he had no fear of the Seminoles raiding his rich plantation holdings and his violent reaction to the St. Augustine Militia's plans to fortify his home. Some early historians believed her to be "the adopted daughter" of Charles Wilhelm Bulow. The family legend goes like this:

Sometime about 1803 Charles Wilhelm Bulow made a trip to St. Augustine, possibly to purchase cattle. He was said to be a friend of King Philip who may have had a Spanish/Indian heritage and was a brother-in-law to Micanopy, an important chief of the Seminoles.

King Philip was the head of the Atlantic Mikasuki Indians. It was said he had a beautiful young daughter. The legend held that a child was born of this daughter. On 16 January 1803 Bulow had married Adelaide Fowler Johnston, a lady of high society in Charleston

How he could have brought an "adopted daughter" and introduced her into the world of Charleston is not known. Emily's 'official' birth date was 20 March 1804. She was later said to be his 'adopted daughter. Emily married William G. Bucknor of New York City on 2 October 1819 listed as an age of 15. She may have been older.

 She had a daughter Elizabeth Bucknor whom I thought had an amazing resemblance to a theoretical great grandfather King Philip in a portrait supplied by Mr. William Lenssen, whose family had a connection to the Bulows.

Wild Cat or Coacoochee was a son of King Philip (Ee-mat-La) and was born in 1810 in Yulaka, a Seminole village on the west side of the St. John's River about 35 miles north of Volusia and the ferry at Picolata. If Emily existed young Coacoochee certainly would have known about his stepsister. He would later make many visits to the Bulow plantation as mentioned in the papers of James Ormond III who was there as a young man.

In 1890 Emily met James Ormond III who spent his last winters in Hotel Ormond, in Ormond Beach Florida. What stories they could tell! The 'fictional' novel **Bulow Gold** tells the legend of Emily the Indian Princess. It remains as a legend. Today a family might exhibit pride in having an Indian heritage but this was not true in the late 1800's.

Emily Bucknor Bulow would inherit all the Bulow lands. No written record exists of this family legend of an Indian Princess, nor is there any historical account of her living at or visiting Bulowville. Several authors of Florida history did list Emily as an 'adopted daughter', thus this tale may have been known by others. Except for some very interesting family photographs in a faded album of William Lenssen, whose family still lives on lands that once were those of the Bulows and who traces his heritage to this family, the tale of an Indian Princess in the Bulow family must remain for our imagination.

30 - The Building of a Plantation

In March of 1821 in Charleston Charles W. Bulow made a will perhaps in anticipation of the dangers of his planned venture. It was a normal will for the times, leaving all to his "beloved wife Abigail Bulow. But if she should not survive then first to his son then to his beloved daughter Mrs. Emily Bucknor, then the wife of William Goelet Bucknor of New York City. A strange part of this will however is a sentence saying "two Negro 'wenches' Mary and Lucy" would be sent first to Abigail and then to Emily. [92] In 1821 the US was beginning to write very repressive slave laws making it difficult or impossible to free a slave. Since Mr. Bullow really commanded hundreds to slaves, not mentioned by name (a survey of his estate after he death did name them) why would he mention only two by name? My conclusion it was a means of freeing them as Abigail did move to New York to live with her daughter. By placing them specifically in his will Charles W. Bulow showed his concern for them.

Bulow's house in St. Augustine was probably in poor condition when he arrived as almost all of the Spanish residents had departed. His attorney John Rodman wrote in 1823: **"Charles W. Bulow on the purchase of said house took possession of the same, and expended a considerable sum of money in repairing and improving the same, and he died in this city in said house, a few months ago."**-*John Rodman executor estate of C. W. Bulow.* [93] The Bulow town house was located next to one of Martin Hernandez (Gen. Hernandez father) and was on Marine Street near the waterfront. (It later may have burned in a great fire of 1914.) Old maps show city docks nearby making movement of household items more convenient if they arrived by boat from Charleston.

There were also records that a Yellow Fever epidemic was present in St. Augustine at this time.

Bulow took title to a Spanish land grant made out to Don Diego Russell (John Russell's son) on 19 June 1821. [94] The father John Russell had died in his daughter's home at

Fernandina after many difficult negotiations with the Spanish to clear his title. A Russell family legend was that the father was mistreated by the Spanish, and perhaps briefly jailed as a British spy.

Now the construction of a great enterprise could begin.

There are no known records on the building of Bulow Plantation. The property most certainly was full of immense long leaf pine trees, heavy undergrowth and fields that had to be cleared to put into production. Various reports say there were 40 to 46 (the number varies in different accounts) slave cabins constructed in a half moon pattern that would surround the main house location. [95] The contents of what would become known as Bulowville is best expressed in a statement made by young John J. Bulow to a notary public on April 1 1836 in St. Augustine, and following the destruction of his works:

Listing of Bulowville properties 2 April 1836:
[96]

This was made by John Joachim Bulow before a notary in St. Augustine following the evacuation and destruction of Bulow Plantation in the Seminole War:

1. A large two story dwelling house $ 5,000

2. Corn-house, barn, poultry-house, and other out-buildings $2,000

3. Two large cotton-houses, one gin-house, stables, two fodder-houses, blacksmith shop, & etc. $4,500

4. Forty Negro houses, all framed, board floors, and shingled $2,500

5. Stone Sugar works, 119 by 93 feet, viz: boiling house-two curing houses, steam engine-house, and a large framed saw-mill, all complete $30,000

6. A large stable, 100 feet long, cooperate and store house $750

7. Household and kitchen furniture $3,000

8. Negro furniture $250

9. *Carpenter's and blacksmith's tools, plantation implements &c. $2,000*

10. *Provisions and stores, Negro clothing, cotton batting, &c. $1,000*

11. *Corn (about 2,000 bushels), fodder, &c. $2,500*

12. *Harness, five ox carts, and two wagons, &c. $250*

13. *Boats, flats, &c. with sails, oars and furniture $250*

14. *Twenty two bales of packed cotton, ready for shipping 7,700 lbs, worth on the plantation thirty-five centers $2,695*

15. *53,000 lbs of stone cotton, equal to 18,000 lbs of clean at thirty-five cents $6,300*

16. *Eight yoke of oxen at $60 $480*

Total $63,475

The crop of the present year at the lowest estimate, would have amounted to $20,000

Total $83,475

At present time we do not know where the miscellaneous buildings in #2 were located.

Francis Pellicer stated he had been the overseer of the plantation for several years past and that the account was just and correct, even understating the value of the anticipated crop. Unfortunately the US Congress never saw fit to honor the Bulow family claim. In January of 1846 it passed the US Senate but failed in the House. The Bulow lands were finally divided by court order in July of 1867 into 8 parcels. Payment by the US government for losses was never made. [97]

One calculation places the loss at over $2,000,000 in 2014 dollars! [98] When you consider that some 300 slaves were brought for its development then the investment becomes huge. In 1821 the price of an "average" slave could be $500 in Spanish gold and for a skilled man such as a carpenter might go up to $1,000 in gold. Thus when some accounts say Bulow moved some 300 slaves from Charleston to begin his works, it represented an incredible amount of wealth being shifted into Florida.

This author believes the construction of quality slave housing was of a high priority in the development of his plantation. He had a fine town house in St. Augustine so perhaps the construction of his plantation house did not come first. Much equipment needed to be ordered including steam engine, kettles, and sugar crushing rollers - - all with long delivery times.

31 - Housing for the Plantation Workers

Coquina sedimentary 'rock' was an important building material in early Florida. It resulted from the combination of tiny shells of mollusks or other ocean dwellers, which are millions of years old, and formed the ancient ocean shores of Florida. When first cut from a quarry, the material is very soft and easy to work. In two to three years it will harden and become almost indestructible. Thus Coquina rock from the nearby ocean would be important. A quarry had to be established with expert stonecutters. This valuable construction material was near the ocean shore. Blocks could be pre-cut to measure for building.

It can be surmised that the early shipments of workers from Charleston contained experts in carpentry, quarrying, stone cutting, shingle making, fireplace building, joining, sawing, lumbering and all the myriad tasks needed to build a new community. They came by ship to Mosquito Lagoon south of the plantation to a place called Live Oak Landing, and thus by small boat up Smith (or Bulow) Creek

We do not know the plan of Charles Wilhelm Bulow for housing his workers but it would be logical that the welfare of his very valuable workers would be important in his planning. James Ormond III had written there were some 300 workers present. [99] Coquina rock would be used in construction.

Thus there were slave houses built with wooden floors, coquina supports and planked walls located in a broad semi-circle around the planned location of the Bulow dwelling house. Each structure was reported to be 12' x 16'. [100] Since the "closure" on the property was not until August of 1821 it would appear that the winter months (where north Florida can become very cold) was close at hand. Further it would be logical that the remainder of 1821 and perhaps 1822 were spent in clearing the property, setting up sawpits for lumber, and supplying the needed materials for construction. Housing of some sort for the workers would be a need.

The semi-circle location of some 46-slave cabins from the main house has been a source of speculation over the years, some researchers saying it was to keep the workers under observation. [101] Others wrote it was a traditional African layout and observed that the Kingsley Plantation in Jacksonville Florida had a similar arrangement of their slave cabins.

Regardless of the motive, the structures were likely very well built and intended to protect the very valuable workers at the plantation. The level of supervision might be explained with the "Task System" of management.

The plans called for 1,500 acres planted for sugar cane, and 1,000 for Indigo dye and rice. Sugar mill machinery at that time could be obtained from the West Point Foundry in Cold Spring, N.Y., Kettles from Scotland's famous Carran foundry, perhaps a high tech Hogden-Holmes cotton gin from Augusta, Georgia and the many other items needed that had long delivery schedules, or came via sail from Europe. In 1822 Bulow purchased a second grant of 2,000 acres from John Addison.

When Charles W. Bulow died in May of 1823 a letter via

fast sail ship must have been dispatched to Paris France, telling young Bulow to return.

We do not know when John Joachim Bulow arrived from Paris. It would be logical that he would first go to Charleston where his uncle John Joachim Bulow (same name) lived with his family. There are records that Mr. Francesco Pellicer (Sr), who was a well-respected Minorcan settler in St. Augustine, and owned a large Spanish grant to the north of the Bulow property, was appointed guardian for young Bulow until he was of proper responsible age.

In 1823 John Joachim Bulow may have been about 16 years old. He possibly did not arrive until that fall allowing time for messages and slow ship transport from France. There likely would be no direct sailings from France to St. Augustine.

Pellicer's son Francesco Pedro Pellicer, [102] about 43 years old, was appointed as a manager of the plantation. He must have been very experienced after working for his successful Minorcan father. Affairs on the Bulow works certainly moved forward rapidly which shows the hand of a good manager. (He was also known as Francis Pellicer.) Pellicer (Sr) held a Spanish land grant south of the Matanzas Inlet, later called Cherokee Grove and today's Princess Place Preserve. He also owned an extensive grant immediately to the north of the Bulow property, thus the development and success of the Bulow plantation sugar works would be of interest to Pellicer also. The strong financial credit of Uncle John Joachim Bulow in Charleston would aid in obtaining the needful things for the plantation. Manager Francis Pellicer also must have done much consultation but unfortunately the letters and correspondence do not exist in the recorded Bulow papers. [103]

Another account was from James Ormond III who as a young man lived briefly on the Bulow plantation in 1828. Ormond wrote that Bulow had a large library of books mostly fiction. He also said Bulow "had about three hundred hands." Since the library was mentioned in 1828, then so likely would the library have existed within a plantation house structure.

"The stone sugar mill was completed according to an inscription set on its north wall reading "Bulow Ville, Jan 26th, 1831." [104] Sugar production may have been much earlier.

"It is not clear where the cane (crushing) mill was located. One description suggests that it was located upstairs in the engine house or on the upper floor of the boiling house. Another more likely possibility is the space between the two structures." [105] **Sweet Cane** by Lucy B. Wayne

32 - The Bulow Plantation House

It may have resembled this. Electronic image by William Ryan

A number of archaeological research projects have been done at the Bulow site, one being in July of 1982. By their study and that of prior researchers it was concluded that the plantation house could have resembled that of the Homeplace Plantation that still exists in St. Charles, Parish Louisiana. [106] It was constructed after 1880. It would have a second story porch or gallery and a large hipped roof that extended over the porch on all four sides. The porch was supported by wood columns, and the roof would contain rooms or sleeping areas.

There might be a brick central heating system on the ground floor extending up through the roof. There could be a wide staircase leading to the second level.

A photograph of the Homeplace plantation showed eight support posts in front; it was surmised that the smaller Bulow house had a frontage of six such support posts as thus the 62 by 42 foot structure would be somewhat smaller than the Homeplace unit. The Louisiana building had a wooden veranda or piazza where the Bulow house also may have had a 10" wide veranda on all four sides of the structure. [107]

Electronic imaging can combine pictures to allow us some idea of what the house looked like.

"I determined the angle of the Louisiana photo and placed my camera as closely as I could to the same height and distance as the known site of the Bulow plantation

house. Using electronic imaging, I colorized the illustration, and placed the support postposition as close to the known ones in the actual Bulow home as I could.

My idea was to show what it looked like when placed on its actual location. I saw that the park artists had used the same building in their signage illustrations at the park."...Bill Ryan.

Artifacts were collected here during several archaeological digs and displayed in a small museum located on the north side of the sugar mill ruins. Amateur collectors or treasure hunters may have removed many artifacts prior to the Bulow works becoming a state park. Some dug here as early as 1914.

33 - Considering Slavery

In 1821 the United States was still very much a nation with slaves although European countries were trying to abolish the practice. Import of slaves had been forbidden in the US since 1808. To the north of Jacksonville were the Zephaniah Kingsley plantations. Charles W. Bulow of Charleston would certainly know of Mr. Kingsley his success as a slaver, planter, plus his management theories. Kingsley had been importing slaves since 1803; he had married one of his African slaves, and had operated very profitable plantation enterprises. Kingsley had very advanced ideas of management structures within his slave population. He believed there must be levels of status within the slave population, where chances of self-betterment could exist.

Looking back some 200 years we must recognize that much of early Florida was built with enslaved Africans, building the roads, the plantations and infrastructure. While freemen also existed in Florida, families had long been escaping to its wilds for their freedom; slavery was an important part of the social and economic times of the plantation structure. The slave and free Negro society during the second Spanish period was much more complicated than many are aware of today. The Spanish had historical codes or rules, they needed free black soldiers for their defense and many favored a three class system whereby African families could change their status, and in some cases by buying themselves, or earning liberty from slavery by services to the Spanish government. The slave could have established rights in the Spanish legal system.

A wonderful study was done by Daniel L. Schafer, for the Journal of Social History 22 March 1993, *A class of people neither freemen nor slaves from Spanish to American Race Relations.* [108] Mr. Schafer relates the complex social and racial structures that existed in Spanish Florida. He explains how the more humanistic Spanish attitude towards their slaves was changed into a rigid one-caste rule when the US took over of Florida in 1821. The concept of free blacks in society began to vanish.

Charles W. Bulow was certainly experienced in slave management as his family had large and successful plantation property in Charleston. He likely would know of Kingsley's concepts of how to effectively organize his enslaved work force.

One concept may have been "The Task System" which was well described in the writings of James Ormond III. It seems much more applicable to wild, hot Florida with its high percentage of African Americans to what might then be the limited numbers of white supervisors:

"Every place had from two to twenty hand-mills of stone to grind the corn and in most places you could hear the mills agoing from half the night as each man or head of the house ground out grist for the next day's grub. The ration was a peck of corn per week. This may seem but poor feed for a man, but it was his bread only, and was ample under the then system of task work. All sorts of labor on the Plantation was portioned out, so much wood to be cut, down in clearing land—so much for grubbing roots—so much in hoeing and harvesting, and so on, so that each one knew in the morning his or her appointed task, and these tasks were so light that an industrious hand could always get through with them by two or three o'clock in the day, and the rest of the time was their own to fish or hunt, or plow or plant as to them seemed best. All had their own little fields or pasture, most of the men owned their own firelocks or guns. Many owned canoes and cast nets, so that on the whole they fared well and were well clad and cared for." [109]

Not every slave owner would have advanced ideas of management for their slave properties. John Bemrose in *Reminiscences of the Second Seminole War* wrote a darker picture of young John Yochim Bulow who appeared following his father's death in 1823. Bemrose likely was in St. Augustine about 1832. John Yochim Bulow was about 25 years old in 1832. Bemrose wrote that the young man, educated in France, did not relate to his slaves, and was callous. He wrote that three slaves were murdered by Bulow.

He further wrote that one killing by young Bulow was when he shot and killed a target marker during a shooting match in St. Augustine much to the dismay of the other planters who placed a heavy fine upon him. [110]

John Bemrose also wrote an unfavorable view of John Bulow's relationship with his slaves accusing him of being "an atrocious slave master then relating a public auction of slaves in St. Augustine.

Bemrose wrote a blistering account of the slave market in St. Augustine. [111] He wrote "Dissipated, and quarrelsome with his equals, tyrannical to his dependents, his hands dyed red with the blood of three of his slaves!" [112]

We do not know how accurate these accounts are as later Bemrose cited a slave chant that was sung while young Bulow "brought his father's body to St. Augustine on his rowing boat." There actually were no direct navigable northern water routes from Bulowville for such a rowing. This also contradicts the Bulow lawyer Rodman who wrote estate papers that clearly state Bulow died in his town house located in St. Augustine. [113]

Bemrose wrote his very valuable account some 30 years after the events when he had returned to England. Editor John K. Mahon pointed out what appeared to be errors in memory by Mr. Bemrose in the University of Florida edition in 1966 of *The Reminiscences of the Second Seminole War*.

It could well be that young Bulow being educated in France and reportedly of a youthful wild nature would not be familiar in the management or value of slave labor forces. However, it could also be surmised that the plantation manager Mr. Pellicer had considerable knowledge, and also experience with his father's efforts. (The Pellicer family also had a large tract of land immediately to the north of the Bulow works in addition to their plantation on what was called Pellicer Creek.)

The Pellicer/John Bulow combination however together did build a great plantation enterprise. Francis Pellicer, plantation manager, must have learned much from his father who had been a Minorcan settler in the failed colony of New

Smyrna. He would know much of slavery and the agony of indentured service from his father, and other local planters. The price of a field slave in 1802 was 300 to 400 dollars of Spanish gold. This might be $9,000 or more today.

When James Ormond III wrote his short account of life on the Bulow plantation he indicated that slaves had "firelocks or their own guns." Accounts do not reveal if this is true. Bulow certainly believed he could defend his own works with his slaves when he violently resisted the entry of the army soldiers. He may also believe his relationship with the Seminoles (the Emily Bulow story) might also be a protection.

The story of Hernandez' mules and slave Luke with his rifle certainly was one of a slave with a rifle. It appeared to me that young Bulow believed his work force could defend his plantation against Indian attack and perhaps had fire arms. The "task system" and its liberal management practices were likely used on the northern Kingsley Plantations. I do not know for certain if it was used at Bulow except for Mr. Ormond's account. It is clear that Caucasian managers on these Florida plantations were not large in number for the quantity of slaves involved. I believe there was a management structure run by slaves on many of these complex and self-sufficient plantations.

The Civil War was not to occur for some 37 years in the future. By 1836 most of these great plantations were wiped out in the Second Seminole War, their slaves scattered, joined with the Indians, or sold. There certainly were smaller plantations opened or re-built here after the disaster of the Seminole war. Slavery was an evil practice. The plantations that grew here could not exist without it. The "slave laws" which removed the limited rights of a slave under the second Spanish period were written after the US take over. The concept of a free man of color vanished after the rule of Andrew Jackson, and in 1838 even those free men in St. Augustine, who ran the many services and shops, were forced to seek out influential white men who would become their "sponsor" or theoretical owner. All persons of color now had to have 'an owner.'

Sugar cane harvest – William Clark 1833 –
Courtesy John Carter Brown Library at Brown University

Only one crop of sugar cane would be raised per year. [114] It was likely an "all hands" operation when the tall canes were to be cut and brought to the crusher.

Because of its great capacity when completed, the Bulow mill may also have done work for the adjacent Pellicer property to the north, and perhaps other planters. Harvest time was normally in November of each year.

The 1830 US Census report for the Bulow Plantation showed a total of 159 persons of which only three were shown as "free white," 5 free colored, and the remainder as slaves.

Only three Caucasian men are shown as possible supervisors. This would indicate that the very complex affairs of the Bulow plantation were managed by some of the slaves. Of the five free colored listed above, three were females. The work force would vary depending on the needs. Bulow could shift workers from the Charleston Bulow plantations as needed so that his number would change as his requirements arose.

SEARCH FOR THE LOST PLANTATIONS OF FLAGLER COUNTY

An engraved block showing BulowVille January 26 1831 was stolen by vandals from the sugar mill but later replaced with a replica. This time may have been during the completion of the existing Bulow Sugar Works, although it is likely the crusher was operating earlier, even with mule or horsepower as was on other plantations.

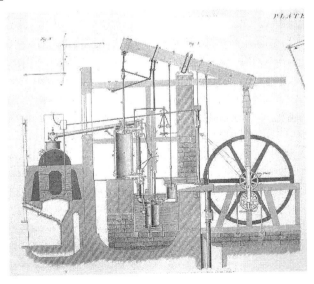

The works included a steam engine, which might have been a Watt 8 horsepower unit similar to one being used at the St. Joseph's plantation to the north. Bulow's machinery was much like that of the older Dunlawton plantation.

34 - Sugar Production at Bulow Plantation Ruins

Dunlawton machinery perhaps similar to the Bulow works -
photo Bill Ryan

The metal at Bulow is gone, sold for scrap. This picture from Dunlawton Plantation further south shows similar equipment which is massive and representative of the new Industrial Revolution that happened with the rapid development of steam engines, castings and machining of complex systems. Bulow had a five kettle 'Jamaica' sugar train in which each kettle was held in a clever construction of firebrick that could deliver increasing heat levels at each vat.

A large, long boiler and furnace filled the right section of the boiler room. Steam was piped to an engine (perhaps on a second floor) that operated a large gear turning and crushing the cane with huge rollers.

Cane was placed on a conveyer that was about three feet wide and lifted it to the roller crushers. The juice then ran below into a settling vat called a Clarifier. Slaked lime was added and a green scum arose to be removed. The crushed cane was called 'Bagasse' and was hauled away in carts.

Picture of sugar line kettle at Dunlawton – similar to Bulow

The juice that flowed from the settling vats went into the 'Grande', which was the coolest of the five kettles, and the furthest from the hot 'Batterie' kettle under which the furnace was fired. This was the hottest. Here was the 'strike' or sugar stage when the juice now undergoing a chemical reaction. It was ladled with wooden scoops into a trough that directed it into large wooden cooling shapes where it hardened.

After hardening it was then spaded into slices, carried in small tubs to the 'purgery' or curing room, and packed in hogsheads.

These wooden barrels were kept in a warm curing room for 20 to 30 days until all the valuable molasses had dripped from the sugar into a cistern located in the recess underneath.

Molasses was sold for making rum.

Illustrations from Bulow Park displays

Shipping took the hogsheads from the floor above the shipping area for loading onto wagons below. Sugar was loaded at the landing for shipment by boat to Jacksonville, St. Augustine or Savannah. Molasses could be sold to Cuban rum makers.

The typical five in line kettles were called 'Grande', 'Propre', 'Flambeau', 'Sirop' and the last was the 'Batterie' which would be nearest the fire. It took great skill with the heavy ladles. Perhaps the workers could observe how slowly juice dripped from their ladle.

A picture of the boiling house of a 'Jamaica type' sugar train drawn on Antigua Island shows the careful transfer of the juice from one heated kettle to another. This highly scientific, industrial process required very skilled labor. The Bulow line was much smaller than this but the principle remained the same.

Illustration by William Clark 1833
Transferring the juice on a Jamaica line
Courtesy of the John Carter Brown Library at Brown University

The Bulow Sugar works is shaped like a T with a joining separate boiler/engine house.

Many of the competitive plantations did not make enough profit in sugar and had gone into debt, but Bulow did prove to be profitable perhaps due to its size and production of other crops including rice, Sea Island cotton, and Indigo.

An excellent description of research on ideas of what the Bulow sugar production facility appeared may be found in the book *"Sweet Cane the Architecture of the Sugar Works of East Florida"* by Lucy B. Wayne. [115]

A sawmill may have been attached to the engine house to benefit from the steam engine's energy during the lengthy times when the sugar mill was not engaged. Sugar production was profitable for the Bulow works. Being able to operate the steam powered sawmill could add additional revenue when sugar was not being processed.

We do not know if they accepted cane from adjacent plantations such as Pellicer, but it seems likely with only one crop per year being available to such a large complex.

Crusher rollers at Dunlawton ruins

Sugar cane crushing rollers from Dunlawton ruins show typical massive construction typical of the steam driven mills. The steam engine and the sugar line would have required wood cut from an entire forest to feed the power of the boiler and the heating system for the sugar line. Unfortunately none of the steam engine works and heavy crushing rollers survived at Bulowville. The ruins of the large Hernandez mill to the north were totally wiped out with the construction of the planned community of Palm Coast Florida.

Bulow Park illustration

Sugar making had to be hot, perhaps dangerous work within the closed boiling house structure but one requiring great skill in knowing when to transfer the heating juice from one kettle to another until the sugar crystallization process had begun. The solidifying sugar juice was now directed into wooden containers where it could be cut into blocks and placed into the hogsheads in the purgery

Sugar making had to be hot, perhaps dangerous work within the closed boiling house structure but one requiring great skill in knowing when to transfer the heating juice from one kettle to another until the sugar crystallization process had begun. The solidifying sugar juice was now directed into wooden containers where it could be cut into blocks and placed into the hogsheads in the purgery

The mill structure was made with carefully cut coquina blocks that required skill, planning and careful placement by the slave quarrymen Coquina rock is soft when first mined but can become very hard in three years' time.

The impressive cut Coquina rock structures still reflect the care and artisanship of the slave stonemasons and quarrymen in the construct of these immense structures. Visiting these ruins can bring history to life after walking the ancient tree lined path from the Bulow plantation house to the sugar mill ruins.

35 - A Dye Stuff as Valuable as Gold

Slaves making indigo in South Carolina from "A map of the Parish of St. Stephen" by Henry Mouzon– courtesy Rare Book, Manuscript, and Special Collections Library, Duke University

For centuries the much-prized blue dye called indigo was obtained exclusively from the indigo plant, and the indigo trade flourished and was prosperous. As early as 1830 a German chemist, Adolf von Baeyer, produced synthetic indigo from coal tar products, but the cost of production was much greater than that of the natural dye.

From then until 1890 he and others worked on the problem of making indigo by less expensive processes and finally succeed in producing it at less than half the cost of the plant dye.

It is believed that the Bulow Plantation and others nearby produced indigo. It was a 'nasty' process with bad smells of fermenting weeds, filtering, capturing the dye flakes. Urine was also used in the process. The cut stems and leaves are crushed and soaked in water for several hours. Fermentation takes place. Then the water, which is clear yellow, is run off into another vat and stirred. Indigo begins to form in bluish flakes on contact with the air and settles. It is filtered through linen, molded into small cakes, and dried for shipment. The image from Duke University shows the process of fermentation, collection and drying the valuable indigo dye cakes that were reputed to be very valuable as part of a plantation's production.

Vegetable indigo comes from a shrubby plant three to five feet high, with rounded leaves and pale red flowers, belonging to the bean family. When three months old and in blossom, the plants are cut down, but soon shoot up again, and yield a second and often a third cutting in one year.

It was written that the small cakes of compressed dye were as valuable as gold. Florida indigo plantations were normally blessed with long growing seasons that enabled the overseers to direct three cuttings of the weed. [116]

It would be likely the process area would be well away from the plantation house due to the bad smells produced in the fermentation process.

It is not known where the Indigo production was located at the Bulow Plantation. The Bulow outbuildings have not yet been located.

A short distance from the Sugar Mill ruin is the Spring House of the Bulow Plantation. It may have been cooled by a flowing artesian well since the water table is close to the surface. The Spring House shows overflow spaces, plus channels to carry off the flow of foul smelling sulfur laden water. Cool water flowing would aid in keeping perishable foodstuffs for longer periods.

The Spring House probably had a wooden roof to protect it from the sun and wooden walls to guard against animal intrusion.

A current listing of priorities has a new protective roof for the Spring House, plus clearing the many years of "muck" from its interior to reveal the original flow of the artesian well

Restoring this spring house is an early project for the Citizens Support Group (CSO) organized by Mr. James Fiske.

36 - Bulow Rice Fields?

In August of 2014 Mr. Chad Light flew his drone aircraft, a DJI Phantom equipped with a camera over the Bulow ruins. This view looking east clearly shows the "Old Road" which ran near the plantation house, crossing on a bridge across Smith or Bulow Creek to provide access to the ocean beach. It might have been on a raised causeway. Accounts wrote that Bulow also raised rice on his plantation. [117] There were opinions this may have happened in this general area. Rice growing requires fresh water, thus on other plantations workers dug up the muck to raise earth barriers or dykes thus allowing a flow of fresh water to leach out any remaining salt. Fresh water could be obtained from nearby holding ponds. Drainage channels holding fresh water would force away the brackish waters and permit the planting of rice. There is the possibility of such drainage areas in these aerial photos, which indicate more research might reveal this was a rice growing area. While it is not known exactly where the Bulow Plantation grew its rice but this general area does correspond to similar areas in Georgia and the Carolinas. [118] The water in Bulow creek is brackish in nature, therefore any rice fields would require a supply of fresh water and dykes to establish this, perhaps also with nearby holding ponds. There appears to be man-made activity in the left side of Mr. Light's aerial photo.

37 - John James Audubon Visits Bulow in 1831

Digital imaging by author

Christmas day 1831 John James Audubon walked south on the King's Road to the Bulow plantation. He had been visiting at Mr. Hernandez' MalaCompra plantation home about 12 miles away. MalaCompra was Joseph Marion Hernandez' country residence and was a cotton plantation.

A picture was created with computer imaging of Audubon resting on the "old road" that today leads to the Bulow Ruins site. It gives an idea of what the King's Road may have looked like. The "old road" would pass the Bulow plantation house, cross the creek behind on a bridge and extended beyond rich rice fields to the Halifax River and ocean.

Audubon was in Florida awaiting transportation by boat to the Gulf Coast and first was in St. Augustine, then travelling south on Old King's road where he would visit with Mr. Hernandez.

I believe Audubon did not find much in common with Mr. Hernandez who would be likely to speak of his plantations then of Audubon's bird project. Hernandez the lawyer and planter had greater interest in crops, falling sugar prices or slaves then would Mr. Audubon.

Audubon was famous for his ***Birds of America*** project. He was in Florida seeking new species to paint. [119]

He was accompanied by Henry Ward, an English taxidermist, and George Lehman a landscape painter.

The famous naturalist was born in Santo Domingo. His father was a French sea captain, his mother a Creole, and he spent time in France. He was about 46 years old that Christmas Day of 1831

John Joachim Bulow was then 24 years old, now very much in control of his great plantation and was surely delighted to receive Audubon. They could speak French since it was their common background.

Bulow had fine wines and the best of food for his visitor. In December 31 of 1831 Audubon wrote: "Mr. J. J. Bulow, a rich planter, at whose home myself and party have been for a whole week under the most hospitable and welcome treatment that could possible be expected, proposed three days that we should proceed down the river in search of new or valuable birds...." [120]

Audubon commented in 1831 that Bulow was erecting some extensive buildings for a sugar house and said the coquina stone could be cut with a common wood axe.

Some accounts tell of Mr. Audubon having to shoot numbers of birds in order to obtain a mounted sample, correct for painting and inclusion in his famous series of birds. "You must be aware that I call birds few when I shoot less than one hundred a day." he wrote

One of his prints hangs in the office of William Lenssen who had family connections to the Bulow history. In this print is presented the only known illustrations of the many Bulow Plantation buildings most of which are not located.

Mr. Lenssen observed that in the winter months the strong and cold nor'easter winds will cause the level of Bulow (or Smith creek as it is called) to suddenly lower. The Audubon trip in the fine deep draft whaleboat [121] with its four rowing stations on each side proved to be almost a disaster as the boat grounded in cold mud, nearly freezing its slave rowers and its occupants. This same boat would later be taken by the army when they occupied the plantation and was lost to the Indians in the disastrous battle of Dunlawton.

Florida in the winter gave a poor impression to the naturalist. His writing indicated there was little to shoot but the many pelicans and herons present, and of course there were many fish in which he was not interested. He wrote that this was not a wonderful place for his visit but commended the excellent hospitality of Bulow.

On January 6th 1832, Audubon and his party returned to St. Augustine from Bulowville, traveling on the King's Highway by wagon and six mules. Many of the live oaks in eastern Florida had been cut down by the "live oakers" [122] who were a type of woodland pirate, not worrying too much about ownership of the very valuable live oak wood so useful in building ships. During his visit he wrote a detailed account of the live oakers. Many of the fine oaks in this part of Florida had vanished including those at Bulow.

While visiting Bulow Audubon collected five hundred fifty bird skins, two boxes of sea shells and did some of his bird drawings. On January 6, 1832, he took a westward trip across the three Haw Creeks to Spring Garden near DeLand. They followed an Indian trail and were accompanied by the engineer whom he wrote built the sugar mill at Bulow. He crossed Sweetwater Creek, which empties into Big Haw Creek and Middle Haw Creek and Little Haw. [123]

Greater Yellow Legs from Audubon's *Birds of America* may show some of the missing buildings on the Bulow Plantation. The view is across Bulow creek looking west.

After visiting with Bulow Audubon toured the camp of the "Live Oakers" Florida's almost pirate oak tree cutters. They were not concerned over the ownership of the trees they cut and sold. He commented on their very hard work in locating and removing the valuable live oak so badly needed in the building of ships.

Many of the slow growing live oaks of Europe had long ago been cut down for building of war ships. Thus the Florida wilderness and its many plantations had very valuable stands of live oak trees that could be cut and sold to the ship builders.

Lumbering would become an important part of the local economy. Since Bulow also had a saw mill, he may have marketed some of his valuable lumber including live oak parts too.

38 - The Distant Thunder of Evil

Re-enactors James Fiske as Francisco Pellicer, James Bullock as slave Scipio [124] and Hewitt Dupont as an 1830 U.S. Army regular soldier brought history alive at the Bulow Ruins State Park. They spoke of possible trouble coming from the new U.S. "Indian Removal" act in Congress. Bulow did not agree to the removal of his Seminole friends who often visited the plantation.

The young United States believed in following its "**Manifest Destiny**" which can be translated as rapid expansion dictated by God, but often at the expense of its native peoples. In the Moultrie Treaty of 1823, signed just south of St. Augustine in what is now called "Treaty Park," the Seminoles were induced to sign away their lands in Florida and move to an interior site where they were to be protected and aided by the U.S. Government. Six of the signing chiefs were bribed by being released from the agreement and given other rewards. Nine years still remained in this "treaty" when Indian Removal was enforced against all Indians.

Andrew Jackson was elected President in 1829 and sponsored a bitterly contested "Indian Removal act" of May 26 1830 saying native people would be removed from the United States to reservation lands to be located West of the Mississippi River. Many broken "treaties" were made with the Indian groups including the "Five Civilized Tribes" that had established towns, churches, farms, and recorded lands of their own. For example the Georgia State legislature cancelled all Cherokee rights to land held in Georgia. The land rush to seize native lands in the United States had begun, as did the desire to capture and sell what were called "escaped slaves" that had lived for long periods in Florida as free men or in relationships with the Seminole Indians.

The darkness of a war was coming to Bulowville and the some sixteen major plantations that were located near the Old King's Road and also in the St. John's river basin.

Profitable production continued on the Bulow Plantation. The relationship with the Seminole Indians remained good. Here is the account of James Ormond III who was living there as a young man:

They had plenty milk butter, and eggs, but for fresh meats depended on the Indian hunters with whom we were on the best terms, and who kept them well supplied with venison and turkies(sp), wild honey and coontie, or arrowroot. Besides which in the fall they would come in with large droves of fat hogs and fat beeves and trade them off for blankets, homespun, powder, lead, red cloths, calico, beads etc at such rates that the cost was but a trifle." Ormond also wrote that the Indian visits often ended "in a big drunk." [125]

Coacoochee or Wild Cat was close to Bulow in age. If John Joachim Bulow were aware of the Emily legend then his adopted sister would be "family" to Coacoochee. Certainly then his relations with the Seminoles would be a good one, and perhaps fortified by strong drink, parties and hunting. The Seminoles were much in the cattle business.

Chief Micanopy reportedly had a herd of more than 20,000 cattle. The planters were the best customers of the Seminole cattlemen. Silver coinage was also valued as much for decoration as for buying things.

The Bulow plantation was very self sufficient, many miles from authority, schools, any stores or other marks of 'civilization.' The yearly crop was in excess of $20,000 (in 1835 dollars) Over a thousand acres were planted in sugar cane and twelve hundred in cotton. molasses, raw sugar, indigo, rice and bales of cotton could be loaded onto flat boats, sent south on the adjoining creek to the Halifax River and then to Live Oak landing were they were transferred to ocean going ships that had arrived in the Mosquito Lagoon. [126]

Two separate kitchens for the plantation house could handle any party or needs of visitors. It was certain that 'Bulowville' was a show place for anyone wishing to visit the wonders of the Plantation world along the King's highway. It was a profitable enterprise. No one believed it could vanish.

The impressive shipping area of the Bulow works can still be viewed today. (Bulow Park illustrations)

39 - Technology, Planning and Dreams Vanish

"Sixteen plantations in Eastern Florida, upon each of which were employed from one to one hundred and fifty Negroes, who built the sugar mills, cotton-gins, store-houses, and dwellings, that were completely destroyed within the month of January 1836; while the occupants fled for their lives, leaving behind the common necessaries of life." [127] (Quote speaks of 'major plantations')

On a very cold dawn the second of January 1836 General Joseph M. Hernandez mounted his horse and led his staff of 22 mostly 'sergeants' down the King's Road from St. Augustine. The bitter Seminole War had begun. On 19 December 1835, he had dispatched a small force under Col. Putnam south in an attempt to secure the plantations and settlers against further Indian attacks. While Bulowville was visited by General Hernandez with his group of soldiers and staff numbering 22 persons, almost every building and many of the Negro houses were occupied by the troops. [128]

"...the General, with his staff and escort left St. Augustine and arrived at St. Joseph's the evening of the same day, which was then occupied as a military post by company D of the 2nd regiment Florida militia. The next day they proceeded to Rosetta and then to Bulowville having fallen in with companies B and C, mounted men, on the road, who had been sent to Bulowville on a scouting party so that the whole group returned to Bulowville." [129]

The Bulow plantation was crowded with soldiers, refugees, slaves and Hernandez' staff. It can be assumed that every slave cabin would be in use, even the large sugar works was occupied as the weather was very cold.

St. Augustine was full of rumors and fears of Indian disasters. [130] Gen. Hernandez needed the truth of things.

He was to visit the works he owned at Bella Vista, Mala Compra and St. Joseph's about 20 miles to the south, and then set up a new headquarters at the rich Bullowville works of John Joachim Bulow. It was now fortified and was held by Major Putnam who had taken his force south from St. Augustine. [131]

Educated as a lawyer, Joseph M. Hernandez was proud of his father Martin who sailed from the Island of Minorca in the Mediterranean, aided an escape from the unsuccessful settlement of Dr. Turnbull at New Smyrna, and then became a well-respected resident of St. Augustine. Joseph Hernandez was born there under Spanish rule.

As part of the plantation aristocracy, he acquired much land and was an important political figure. When the Americans took over in 1821, he was the delegate from Florida to the US Congress and the first Hispanic. Hernandez knew a Seminole War was coming and had done much to recruit a defense. He was named as a general of the then unprepared Militia in East Florida.

The Second Seminole War would soon reduce the plantations of East Florida into burned rubble. What the war had failed to erase, the later development of Florida would wipe away. The King's Highway built by the British before the American Revolution slowly vanished. On Hernandez's trip the King's was now a rough, sandy trail even then it was no longer the smooth stagecoach route of the British era.

His soldiers would travel this road many times during the war.

Many visitors have strong feelings for the Bulow plantation ruins. As you stand here in the deep silence of the woods you feel history. Bulow Plantation Ruins seem far away from the sound of traffic and modern Florida. The impressive ruins show the craftsmanship of the slaves that cut and placed these closely fitting blocks. Can you sense the events that happened here so long ago?

This place carries a story it led me to write a book called *"Bulow Gold"* which although fictional, I say to you it can speak within its silence.

Use your imagination to see and feel some of the rich Florida history that echoes faintly in a few places that still retain the memory of these destroyed and almost forgotten lost plantations. Stand here and admire the carefully cut and fitted coquina stones, some now blackened by fire. Reflect on the slave engineers that ran the steam engine and the skilled artisans that made sugar, and operated this complex place.

40 - The Causes of War

What historians call "The Second Seminole War" would last for seven bloody years with some 1,500 dead soldiers and militia. It ended with the US army declaring victory in 1842, and then later going off to fight in Mexico in 1846. Like many wars it originated from common reasons; greed for land and unfair treatment of the Native Americans, complicated with slavery, slave escapes into Florida, and the "Black Seminoles."

The many plantations along The King's Highway had previously good relations with the Indians who were their prime customers and traders for their beef, venison and occasional labor. After the Moultrie treaty, harsh laws were being enacted forbidding Indians to leave from their "reservation." The Seminoles were now greatly reduced and often in poverty.

Andrew Jackson who had defeated the Indians in The First Seminole War was elected President in 1829. There were at the time some five 'Civilized Tribes' that owned large amounts of land, had well established societies but whose ownership of land under the harsh Indian Removal Act now would no longer be recognized.

"Who was an Indian and who was a slave?" was complicated by families that had escaped from the north for over a hundred years. Called as Maroons or Black Seminoles they had long-standing, strong relationships with Seminole Indians. While these escaped slaves were few in number, they were a sore point with the Georgia and Carolina planters. When their slaves might know of a place where they could escape was a bitter one to slave owners.

Osceola His Capture and Seminole Legends, is a book I wrote to give Seminole leader Osceola in a position to tell his story in a first person narrative. (In real life Osceola did not write any account and reportedly was not fluent in English)

The many meetings, treaties, and efforts by the Indians

to avoid conflict were recorded. Some Chiefs saw that it was a war they could not win. They agreed to be transported. Others believed war was certain and began to prepare. Osceola, while not a chief, would later become a 'War Leader' and agitated for action in its early days until he was captured under a white flag of truce as related in the "Osceola" book. The Second Seminole War was beginning. (The first was Jackson's war) In late 1835 and near Christmas Eve there were a series of attacks on plantations in Florida by the Seminoles. Refugees fled up Old King's or boated up Smith or Bulow Creek, where many ended up at Bulowville. While exact events at Bulow's Plantation are not known, it was observed by many authors that Bulow was very opposed to the U.S. army occupying his property. General Putnam later wrote to the U.S. Congress: "It is well known that the Indians of Florida were at peace with the white inhabitants of that territory and that the friendliest intercourse existed between them when the policy of removing them west of the Mississippi was adopted by the United States Government."
132

41 - The 'Mosquito Roarers'

Indian unrest was now all over Florida. Important planter Joseph M Hernandez held a commission in the Florida Militia. He petitioned the Secretary of War urgently for some 500 muskets. Joseph Hernandez was named as a Brigadier General Commanding the militia (2nd Regiment, 2nd Battalion) in Florida. He was owner of three plantations near Bulow, Bella Vista to the far north, Mala Compra Plantation, where he had a house, and St. Joseph, which was the largest, all bordering the Matanzas River. The very nervous authorities in St. Augustine were collecting all hunting rifles or arms from their local free black residents who now were being viewed with worried eyes. [133] Rumors were they were supplying arms and food to the Indians. Unknown to them at the time Maj. Francis Dade and his army group had marched out of Fort Brooke (near present Tampa) to re-enforce the soldiers at Fort King to the north. This was the end of December 1835, probably around the 24th. The 'friendly chiefs' who had taken refuge at Fort Brooke watched them depart probably knowing the danger the soldiers faced in a trip into the Seminole heartland. On Monday December 28, they met a strong Seminole force with the result now being called "Dade's Massacre." [134] Attacks were happening throughout Florida.

  Also on 28 December Gen. Thompson and a friend Lt. Constantine Smith were riddled with rifle bullets outside Fort King (today known as Ocala) by Seminole warriors directed by Osceola. The war had begun.

  On December 17 Gen. Hernandez had dispatched army units to protect plantations to the south. The group of Maj. Putnam went by way of Mala Compra plantation, St. Joseph's and then to Rosetta, the plantation of the Marquis DeFougiers where he was to make a headquarters. Enroute they made a short stop at the entrance to Bulowville where Gen. Putnam said Bulow was "most uncivil" when mounted companies B & C were sent as scouts. At this time it was reported "there were strong words" between Lt. William

Williams, who was the son of army general Williams, and Bulow relative to the prospective occupancy of troops.

Affairs were closing in rapidly with anticipated large forces of hostile Indians, plantations burning, and desperate refugees. Most of the inhabitants of the Halifax region had collected at Bulowville, frightened to go further without protection. [135] Gen Putnam thus decided to return to Bulowville at night on December 28 from his camp at Rosetta. At Bulow he could make a defendable fortification. Bulow reportedly was enraged and fired a four pound cannon charged with powder at the soldiers. We can imagine this happening on "Beach Road" which was the approach to the plantation from The King's Road with the horses rearing and men taking cover from the blasts of the small cannon.

One soldier present, Mr. C. Downing, gave testimony at a Senate Hearing:

"...and so rude was he in the reception of the officers, that they book possession of his house, and would not admit him to their mess, at his own table."

"He was pressed as a soldier, and, it is said put under guard for his opposition to this military occupancy of the premises; nay, more: when the post was about to be abandoned, Bulow's wagons, carts, and teams were all pressed to carry the soldier's baggage, and it is said he was not permitted to put into them a single article." [136]

For many years local searchers with metal detectors and diggers searched the Bulow Ruins for the "Bulow Gold" with rumors of it re-appearing. Digging or using electronic devices is now strictly prohibited in a state park. Several accounts by soldiers who returned after the plantation was burned, said Bulow's fine library was blowing across the fields.

Since the house was burned and normally the library would be in flame, this might indicate that 'something' was buried for protection and later dug up by the Seminole Indians. It was clear that Bulow was not permitted to take anything from his plantation when it was abandoned by the army.

If his books were lying about outside and did not burn

with the house, could this mean that his "gold" was buried too?

Who would be most likely to find anything hidden and dig it up but the Seminoles who were familiar with the plantation and Bulow?

Once the plantation was fortified by the army and abandoned it was game for destruction.

The bitter Second Seminole War drained the US treasury until August 24th of 1842 when the President of the United States announced that hostilities had ceased. For the Seminoles that still remained in Florida, it was a war that never really ended. Seminole villages were destroyed by the army. Log cabins, store houses, meeting houses were burned and lost.

(Bulow park illustration shows possible structure of army fort)

Bulow slaves were told to pile Cotton bales around the periphery of the Bulow house. Then they cut logs to complete a fort with water well in the center. The work was aided by Bulow's teams of oxen to haul in the hastily cut logs. When the Bulowville plantation was converted into a fortress by the army large breastworks were built, 40 feet square with angles at the corners, about 10 feet high, made of heavy cabbage logs. Bulow oxen teams were put into this hard usage as were his workers. All outbuildings including slave quarters were now occupied by the army. [137] We suspect his store of fine wines and food was rapidly vanishing with the army's occupation.

42 - The Battle of Dunlawton

Soldier John S. Williams gave later testimony to the US Senate: *"The only property which appeared to have been destroyed by the Indians, upon any of the plantations at Matanzas within a district of 30 miles, was such as had been occupied, or to some extent fortified by the Military."*[138] This belief was also supported by later statements of Gen. Hernandez. As the war continued the destruction was greater. Untouched Florida properties were eventually broken into rubble.

Apparently John Bulow had some justification for believing his Indian friends would not attack his plantation, or at least he could hold onto it with his large number of slaves, some of whom had hunting fire arms. His fury at the army's occupation did result in his firing his small cannon at them, perhaps to startle their horses as they approached on the narrow" old road."

Open, planted fields of sugar cane probably existed beside the "old road" that now runs from the 'Old King's Road' to the Bulow Plantation. In 1835 the trees and heavy brush to the north probably did not exist, being replaced by cleared areas, but the road likely looked much the same.

Food was running out at Bulowville and water supplies were doubtful. On January 23, 1836 General Putnam decided to take a detachment of troops south to the Dunlawton Plantation where he believed some corn or food stuffs might be obtained. Putnam took some 25 of his 40 men using Bulow's boats including his fine rowing whaleboat and two large canoes for the exploration south to Dunlawton Plantation.

They first went to Mrs. Anderson's plantation on the Halifax but were informed by a Negro that all was burned. On arrival that night they found that some of the houses were burning. The soldiers concealed within the ruins of two slave houses, near to a pen, which held cattle possibly for the Indians the next morning.

They had begun to salvage what food they could.

James Ormond III, who was present, made this comment:

"The whole command was just an undisciplined rabble, under no command of their officers, not a man had ever before seen a gun fired in anger.

The houses were still on fire,--that is, the dwellings on the river bank, the mills were a mile or more back from the river. The first thing we in our boat saw was some of our men had gone ashore and were engaged in chasing the chickens around the burning houses."

In the morning two Indians were seen approaching the site where the solders had spent a very restless night.

"Messrs. Anderson and Douglas Dummitt, who were keeping guard; these gentlemen fired, one of the Indians fell, and the other was wounded. Mr. Dummitt ran to the fallen one and as he was stooping over him, there was a report of rifles, and he received a wound in the back of his neck; a large body of Indians immediately after rushed out of scrub, about musket shot distance and commenced a furious attack."

A fierce fire fight went on for about an hour. It looked like there were too many Indians and they rushed back to the boats. Their guns were now wet and would not fire. The creek had also lowered making some crafts aground in the heavy mud. Coacoochee or Wild Cat had appeared on horseback now leading the very angry Indians.

James Ormond III gave perhaps the best description of the battle, although many including Dan Dowling wrote vivid accounts. His actual words give the best description of Wild Cat during the confusion and desperation of that battle: "He mounted on a white or grey horse in full war paint or costume and with the reflectors from the Mosquito Bar Light House which they had burned a few days before, as a head ornament, came charging down on us."

"Maj. Putnam's company, though so inferior in number, kept them off for the space of an hour during which the firing was sharp on both sides. The Indians, however, began to flank and surround them, and their situation was getting dangerous and desperate."

Ormond tells of the wild rush for the boats amid a hail of Indian bullets. Only one man was immediately killed, whom he identified as "Will" a slave of John George Anderson. Several accounts of the battle indicate that the small caliber of the Indian rifles and their hasty loadings kept the hits from being worse.

"Domingo Martinelli was shot under the right shoulder and later died of the wound. Domingo Usina was shot in the back and died of the wounds after some years of suffering. Julius Reynolds of Wadnalaw Co. Carolina was shot just under the right eye. I got four balls—one in my left side, in the 'barr' of my ear, one in the right shoulder and lodged alongside my spine where the doctor cut it out." - - Ormond Ben Wiggins, a colored guide had shown great bravery and was sorely wounded.

Mr. M.M. Cohen wrote in 1836 that Pvt. Sheldon was hit in the forehead, between his eyes. The wound certainly would have been fatal, he said, except that the Indians were loading their rifles rapidly without the needed patch to seat the small caliber ball.

"The first discharge of an Indian rifle is generally fatal; afterwards they load carelessly and hurriedly. The weapon to be efficient, must be charged with care; but the Indian fills his mouth with bullets, pours the powder from his horn into the barrel, then spits the ball into the muzzle, causing it to roll down without patch or ramrod, then, between whoops and frantic gestures, seeks an opportunity to fire."

Col. Putnam was hit. Ambrose Cooper's arm was broken by a rifle ball, in all some reports said three were killed and fourteen wounded out of the 25 soldiers that had rowed so bravely down to Dunlawton.

James Ormond III also relates a worse problem when the Indians were able to launch the abandoned whaleboat to pursue the fleeing soldiers whose guns were now wet and had only one fire piece that might shoot. He wrote that the one gun that would still shoot produced a lucky shot that skipped on the water, made a hit on an Indian in the whaleboat. When he fell into the water, the other Indians gave up the chase. Sadly two young men tried to reach the beach and from there safety at Bulow. Ned Gould and George Marks tried but Gould was taken and likely killed.

Testimony to the long range of the Indian rifles was an account of Lt. William Williams, a son of General Williams, and who previously had an argument with Bulow. He had pulled off his pants to wade and called out a taunt. A nearly spent ball hit him in the rear making a painful impression, from which Mr. Ormond offered little sympathy.

Some 17 of the 25 (some accounts wrote 40) soldiers who had bravely rowed to Dunlawton were now placed in the Bulow plantation house as it served as a hospital. Some had such severe wounds they were not expected to live.

Benjamin Putnam who was also wounded expressed his state of mind in a statement made later to a US Congressional hearing in February of 1843.

"*After the battle at Dunlawton, we had every reason to think the Indians would pursue us by land, and occupy positions on the side of Smith's* creek, through which we were obliged to pass with our boats. This creek is about ten miles in length, and very winding and narrow; and the west side might have been occupied very advantageously by the Indians; and if they had done so, they must have destroyed my* *whole detachment, as there were no means of escape and we could have offered but a very feeble resistance in our disabled condition. We left the post, when we abandoned it after dark, as it was deemed more safe to do so at that time than by day."* [139] ***Smith's Creek is now called Bulow Creek. It likely appears as it did in 1836.***

Brave army messengers went up and down the King's Road to Gen. Hernandez headquarters in St. Augustine. With the belief that large groups of Indian warriors were closing in, and perhaps cutting off the army, orders were sent to evacuate Bulowville, even though a very strong fort was built there and perhaps could have been defended. A lack of food, sickness, and the serious wounds of the group who fought at Dunlawton most likely aided the decision.

43 - Were They 'Taken' or Did They Join?

Refugees and their slaves kept appearing at Bulowville although their numbers are unknown. Many writers of the time indicated that valuable plantation slaves were being "taken" by the raiding Seminole Indians. Written accounts then did not describe the plantation slaves "revolting" or joining with the Seminoles, as had "The Black Seminoles" those who had a long relationship with the Indians and had adopted their culture after living in Florida for a long period of time.

Later claims for losses at the burned plantations did mention valuable slaves "**taken by the Indians.**" These were considered part of their financial loss and later claims for reimbursement from the government. (Most were later refused in the Congress)

Were they taken or did they join?

Professor J.B. Bird in his website *johnhorse.com*, and other researchers believed that written histories of the time hid what they named "**The largest slave rebellion in U.S. history**" as being one that was concealed since the United States was then very much a slave country. It would be dangerous for the slaves in Georgia, the Carolinas, Virginia, and Mississippi to discover that slaves joined with Indians in Florida and fought the U.S. army to a near halt.

Professor Bird's historians tabulated the slave losses from 18 attacked Plantations and arrived at the number 416 as those slaves claimed as "taken." The "Black Seminoles," those who had long lived with the Indians, were known fierce fighters. While records that show how many slaves really joined with the Indians and their Maroon partners to take up arms are thin, such action did happen in the early days of the Seminole War. The Seminoles were not equipped to feed and house slave families and the Indian culture were very different from those who had lived in the ordered world of the Plantation. Plantation manager Pellicer reported that Bulow lost only four "prime Negroes" named George, July, Scipio and Abraham. So perhaps four of Bulow's "prime men" did join with the Indians. A later tabulation of Prof. Bird showed that Hernandez lost only three. Was this because conditions did not favor escape or was it that both Plantations were abandoned but not directly attacked, or perhaps a slave's choice of the lesser of two evils?

See: johnhorse.com/highlights/essays/largest.htm

This research work, found on the Internet, cites the references concerning the escaped slaves that took up arms. We have only a few written hints eg. The account of James Ormond III as to the nature of slavery at the Bulow Plantation. The numbers seeking refuge at Bulowville plus those slaves living at Bulow must have been large. Feeding and housing a large group in the winter would have been a serious problem.

Dan J. Dowling wrote a differing observation in 1836:

"...the event has shown that a large majority of our slaves preferred to remain with their masters in the happy and secure state of servitude to which they had been accustomed, rather than to seek a better one in a visionary and uncertain independence, and exemption from toil, in which they would still be subject to domination of another sort—to the lawless caprices and cruel power of some savage tyrant, to cares and privations, and numberless other ills."

This Southern point of view might be accurate as the choices available to a slave were few.

Slaves "were taken" or joined voluntarily with the Seminole raiders as outlined in Prof. Bird's research. It would be a difficult decision to depart from the known life on a plantation to join a very different Indian culture.

General Jesup certainly knew the peril of the black

warrior in Florida. He wrote this upon taking command of the army in Florida on December 9, 1836:

"This, you may be assured, is a Negro, not an Indian war; and if not speedily put down, the South will feel the effects of it on their slave population before the end of the next season."

Jesup knew of the effect that a successful slave revolt in Florida would have in the South. There had been other revolts, put down violently, but none with the numbers that were then happening in Florida. He later made many plans to separate the Black Seminoles and any escaped slaves from their Seminole warrior partners, and in this he was mainly successful by offering a certain "freedom" if slaves were sent west as Seminole 'property.'

Gen. Jesup later made many maneuvers in negotiations intended to separate the Black Seminoles and escaped slaves from their Seminole Indian allies. He did agree to offer some kind of "freedom" to those going West to Indian Territory when he defined them as "Seminole property."

Bulow Plantation is abandoned

On 23 January 1836 Gen. Putnam followed orders to abandon Bulow. Every cart, wagon, and linked oxen with carts were prepared. To make the wounded more comfortable beds and mattress were taken from the plantation house. Their guard for the night time trip did not exceed 55 men who were still "effective" against unknown numbers of hostile Indians. A description of their trip appears in the book "***Bulow Gold***" which while historical fiction; may have accurately recorded the event:

"*The night was a terror. The ox carts groaned, men were coughing or moaning. The iron shod wheels cracked and popped over the pieces of crush shell on the old roadway. In some place there was water ankle deep over the road. Everyone expected the high war cry of the Seminole at any moment. Our long column stretched far into the blackness. We had two large wagons pulled by four horses each. The three large carts once used to carry sugar can were* pulled by yoked oxen. There was a long procession of walking slaves and white refugees.

In this fear and confusion came young Bulow with only the clothing he wore. The richest, most successful planter in all Florida walked in darkness carrying nothing that was his. We arrived at the St. Joseph Plantation about 3 in the morning, all very tired and hungry. Hernandez' large store house still had rich supplies of corn, pumpkins from his fields plus supplies that had been sent there for the soldiers."

The wounded soldiers were sent onward to St. Augustine by boat. The large column of plantation slaves went to Anastasia Island near St. Augustine into a camp set up for that purpose.

Bulow's oxen, wagons and horses may have been abandoned with the Hernandez St. Joseph's plantation as they were later listed as "lost" in the Bulow estate claim.

"About the 27th of January all of the slaves from Bulow's, Williams', Dupont's, Hernandez' and other plantations were sent to Anastasia Island were city authorities directed they be located." [140]

44 - The Slave Camp at Anastasia Island

Historical accounts are silent on what became of the Bulow slaves in their camp near St. Augustine. Certainly others from the many destroyed plantations numbering about 300 and those from smaller farms were mixed in. St. Augustine was packed with refugees, in a high state of panic with the former plantation owners now refugees themselves, perhaps not able to provide the food or housing for their once very valuable workers.

Image Library of Congress

It was also noted that temperatures were very low. In the winter of 1835 there had been an exceptional freeze, and the winter of 1836 was harsh too. With only makeshift shelter they may have suffered greatly. Their owners were refugees too and would hardly be able to provide the food, clothing and housing needed for a bitter winter climate. [141]

Jessie Fish once had extensive property on Anastasia Island and perhaps the ruins of his works played some role of shelter for the large numbers of slaves sent to Anastasia.

A hint lies in Alice Strickland's account of the Dummett plantation: **"The Dummetts took their slaves with them to St. Augustine, and they did not run away to join the Seminoles, as some others had done. The confinement of town life was disastrous to the Dummett slaves, unfortunately and twenty-five of** them sickened and died –mostly from tuberculosis, which had been unknown on the plantation." [142] "Many of the negro slaves of the Florida planters deserted their owners and joined the Seminoles at the beginning of hostilities but the Dummett's slaves remained loyal. However, some of them were taken off by the Indians and this loss, together with the destruction of the plantations resulted in Colonel Dummett having to sell the remainder of his slaves, who, nevertheless, always retained their affections for the family." [143]

Slaves were much in demand in the cotton and rice plantations in Georgia and the Carolina and while records do not show this, it can be assumed that many were sold from the Anastasia camp and never returned to Florida.

We speculate that many were later sold to the cotton growers in Georgia or the Carolinas where conditions were far less favorable than those in Florida. Like the plantation owners they now had lost their position if they had one in the slave community and would be fearful at to what the future would bring including terrible events of separated families, or even death due to harsh living conditions at St. Augustine's Anastasia Island slave camp.

Hernandez did rent out some of his slaves from the Anastasia camp to the City of St. Augustine. At the end of the Seminole war he also sent some slaves back to MalaCompra in an attempt to begin again. [144]

The Seminole war had to be an equal disaster for the slave families of the now destroyed plantations. They faced a new and uncertain future in faraway places.

Hagerstown Mail March 4 1836
(Photocopy from Flagler County Historical Society)

The Indian War

The St. Augustine Herald of the 15th inst, states, that the whole of the country south of St. Augustine, has been laid waste during the previous week. There is not a single house now remaining between that city and Cape Florida, a distance of 250 miles; all, all, have been burned to the ground.

On Sunday morning, the 14th Feb., a dense smoke was seen in the south, in the direction of Bulowville, and it was conjectured that the buildings on that plantation were in flames, and it was known that there were none but Indians in that direction. The smoke was seen in the same direction on Tuesday. On Thursday, it was reported that General Hernandez's houses at St. Joseph's were on fire, and in the afternoon, this report was confirmed by two of General Hernandez's Negroes, who stated that they had rode from Mala Compra to St. Josephs, that morning, and came within a quarter of a mile of the houses and had a full view of the burning buildings.

They state the houses to have been fired about 7 o'clock that morning and that every house except the corn house was burning at the time they were there. The Indians had posted sentinels at some distance from the houses; while the main body was dancing around the fire. The Negroes can give no correct idea as to the number of Indians, but say that there was a large crowd of them.

The Plantation of Col. James Williams was also set on fire and destroyed at the same time. Mr. Dupont's plantation of Buena Retires is also destroyed. There now remains no doubt of the destruction of Bulowville. It is of the opinion of many that after the battle of Dunlawton, the Indians procured a large reinforcement and returned to attack Bulowville. The amount of property destroyed is immense, at Bulowville alone, the buildings are said the have cost 50,000 dollars. The property destroyed last week on these plantations cannot be less than 200,000 dollars.

Extract of a letter, from a member of the Light Infantry Volunteers to a gentleman of Charleston, S.C. dated - -St. Augustine, Feb 14

"What I told you in my last, as founded upon rumor, has proved to be fact: Bulow's, Hernandez's, and some other places have been entirely devastated, and beyond doubt, the *enemy is within a few miles of us. Last night an alarm was made at the upper piquet, and our company was the first upon the ground. The men acted promptly, and appeared anxious to meet the foe. Our officers showed that they know their duty, and the calm, but energetic movements of our Captain drew forth the admiration of every man of the corps. When we arrived at the piquet station where the alarm was given a portion of the company were placed under Lieut. Jervey, to strengthen the sentinels, and on his return we scoured the adjoining wood under Capt. Ravenel. Nothing was discovered, but it is presumed that a scouting party of the enemy gave cause for the alarm as the sentinels who first fired were men who could be depended upon.*

At half past 12 we returned to the barracks, and had no further occasion to be called out. A scouring party has just returned, and reports that they saw tracks, which did not belong to our men. Before you receive this the South-Carolina troops will be here, and Gen. Scott is anxiously expected every day. We have no more news from Camp King. An express arrived yesterday from Picolata, who stated that the night previous a sentinel fired and moccasin tracks were seen."

St. Augustine, Feb 15

"It is rumored in the city, that an attack was made on the outer Piquet on Saturday night last—there were 15 muskets fired at the Indians, without effect. We expect an attack every night from the enemy—should they attempt it, they will meet with a warm reception." [145]

St. Augustine was full of rumors and fear. On January 9, 1836 members of the Llenovar family were murdered just outside the city gates. Refugees were arriving daily all with stories of Indian attack and destruction that caused much fear.

A good view of affairs in St. Augustine at the time of Bulow's arrival can be found in a rare book *Sketch of the Seminole War and Sketches during a campaign* written by Dan J. Dowling in August of 1836:

"To add to the alarm, which at this time prevailed generally throughout the territory, it became to be no longer doubtful that there was an understanding between the Seminoles and Creeks, which had been anticipated and feared. To what extent the Creeks were hostile, was not yet ascertained. On the 19th, it was rumored that 500 Indians, supposed to be Creeks were encamped on the north side of the St. Mary's river in Georgia. (The Creeks numbered about 7000 warriors and were a powerful and warlike nation.) Thus, there was speculation about a new Indian War involving both the Creeks and the Cherokees who were known to be averse to removing."

Many rumors and fears of destruction were haunting the citizens of St. Augustine. Some were upset when the small force of Gen. Putnam went south to defend the planters and confront the Indians. Rumor of slaves supplying Indians caused a collection of all fire arms held by free Negroes within St. Augustine, and many new rules restricting their movements

45 - An Indian Camp on Haw Creek

On the three fords of Haw Creek that feed into Dunn's Lake (Crescent Lake) of Flagler County is a site that could be the lost camp of Halleck Tustenuggee. [146] Near the end of the Seminole conflict, he raised total war on the white settlers leaving a trail of death across murdered settlements from Espanola to St. Augustine. In December of 1841, he raided Mandarin near St. Augustine killing settlers and then vanishing.

Col. Fanning and Maj. Ashby sketch map 1838 shows Indian camps (smoke rising) on the 3rd ford of Haw Creek. This could be the lost camp of Halleck Tustenuggee. The Spring Garden trail ran through it to connect with Old King's Road further north.

Seat of War 1839 Map of Capt John McKay and LT. E. Blake showing the Haw Creek area.

The Volusia to St. Augustine "Spring Garden" trail connects to King's Road in the northeast. This is an ancient Indian route and was reportedly used by leader Osceola when he travelled to meet with the army at St. Augustine.

Halleck Tustenuggee was violently opposed to the army's occupation of Florida and reportedly killed his own sister when she had talked about surrender. He took part in many violent battles and had been wounded at Fort King. Sprague in "The Florida War" wrote about the attacks made by Halleck after his recovery: *"The attack upon the settlement of Mandarin, twenty miles south of Jacksonville, on the eastern bank of the river St. John's and thirty-five miles from St. Augustine on the 29th of December, counterbalanced all that was realized at Fort Brooke. This marauding party consisted of seventeen men, belonging to the band of Halleck-Tustenuggee. They came from the neighborhood of Dunn's Lake and Haw Creek."*

Sprague wrote that two men, two women, and an infant were killed. Since the army had believed the Seminole war was almost over, there was great panic among settlers and a strong effort made to locate this Indian raider. [147]

The army had long sought this elusive raider and patrolled Graham's and Bulow's swamps, Tomoka River, Spring Garden until they came upon the camp on 25 January 1842.

They traced the Halleck Tustenuggee group to the Haw Creek area. His warriors totaled 35 men, mostly Miccosukee. A strong battle ensued between the army raiders and the Indians.

"Though the command was for some time exposed to the unceasing fire of the enemy, secreted in a dense hammock, but one man was killed and two wounded. The stand here taken was to cover the retreat of the (Indian) women and children who were one day in advance." [148]

The Indian warriors vanished into the thick brush and the army searched for a lengthy period to locate them again.

When the army searched the camp they found a large cache of supplies including powder kegs, cloth, cotton, blankets and calico buried in the earth, hollow trees and small palmetto sheds. [149]

On April 19, 1842, Halleck and his band were finally captured. He was sent west to Indian Territory. During the Civil War, he assisted the Federal Government and led his Seminole warriors in three battles after which they had to retreat to Kansas where he probably died.

On August 14, 1843, Col Worth of the US army announced that hostilities with the Indians of Florida had ceased. [150]

A September 1976 news article reported that Otis Hunter, then a County Commissioner had long searched the area for Indian relics and reported on an area south east of

Espanola called "War Paint Hill" where varicolored clay could be obtained for decorating the Indian warriors.

These well-armed raiders had caused much fear in what would become Flagler County during the Seminole war and had remained hidden in their Haw Creek encampment until January of 1842. They may well have participated in the burning of the lost plantations of Flagler which had begun that Christmas Eve of 1835.

Flagler historian and author Jack Clegg with library director Doug Cisney visited the beautiful Haw Creek area at the *Haw Creek Preserve* (Russell Landing). It was surmised that this location may be close to the lost camp of Halleck-Tustenuggee.

This remarkable park with its boat launch area in western Flagler County is virtually unknown and rarely visited. It is located at the "navigable" section of Haw Creek that leads to Dunn's (Crescent) Lake by way of "Dead Lake." It is believed that Indian groups camped here for a very long time, and raised their crops of maize.

46 - May 7, 1836: Death of John Joachim Bulow

The grave of his father Charles Wilhelm Bulow lies in the "Huguenot" graveyard near the north city gate of St. Augustine. There appears to be an empty spot next to it. Perhaps this spot holds the answer to a mystery concerning the son John Joachim Bulow.

Here are some facts; you must make your own judgment, as history remains silent. My own feelings differ with the 'official accounts' but here they are:

In April of 1836 John Jacob Bulow was alive. He was collecting statements as to his loss before a notary. His name is listed in the documents.

"April 1st 1836 St. Augustine Florida – Sworn to before me at St. Augustine. St. John's county, Florida this 2nd day of April A.D. 1836 George D. Phillips Justice of the Peace.

I Francis Pellicer, solemnly swear that I have been for several years last past the overseer of Mr. J. J. Bulow, Jr.'s

plantation Bulowville, at Tomoka, Mosquito County, and East Florida. That I am well acquainted with every transaction that has taken place on the plantation, am conversant with the quantity, value, and cost of everything thereon...."
Francis Pellicer

Following was a detail listing of the plantation assets of John J. Bulow, Jr. totaling some $83,475 in 1836 dollars.

On April 2^{nd,} some of the "Mosquito Roarer" militia also gave sworn statements as to the seizing of the plantation. These included Joseph Hunter, William H. Williams, and David R. Dunham. They said the $20,000 estimate for crop potential was conservative and probably would have amounted to more.

Then were given statements by Maj. Benjamin A. Putnam and Joseph N. Hernandez Brig. General 2nd Brigade Florida Militia who wrote the plantation was occupied, and fortified under their direction. These were all part of Bulow's claim which was before the notary.

Thus John Joachim Bulow, Jr. was alive on 2 April 1836 and getting some cooperation from the men who had sized his plantation, and locked him up. At this time, Bulow was still a very wealthy man. His slaves were at Anastasia Island, and his uncle, his financial supporter remained in Charleston. He still owned the town house in St. Augustine and while he had to walk up the King's Highway at night with only the clothing he wore, he almost certainly had assets in St. Augustine, or with his uncle in Charleston. His uncle' John Joachim Bulow owned a fine house at the corner of King and Cannon streets in Charleston with many slaves. The uncle will not die until 23 June 1841. [151] The City of St. Augustine was in great confusion. Indian attacks were expected at any moment, and the stories of the refugees and plantation owners grew with each telling.

The news of the Dupont plantation raid would have happened early on Saturday May 7th. The Militia certainly rode out that day to do battle and returned that evening to St. Augustine. The militia men would not be in a happy frame of mind having lost friends and engaged in a shoot out.

Violent times were happening around St. Augustine. Here is a hint of a motive for the sudden demise of Bulow. Ruth Danenhower Wilson wrote *The Bulow Plantation, 1821-1835* for the Florida Historical Quarterly in 1945:

"What became of the spoiled young man whose life had been so suddenly changed by the fortunes of war little is known beyond the bare fact of his death three months later on May 7, 1836?"

Some authors had John Joachim Bulow returning to Paris where he would die from a 'broken heart." [152] This was hardly likely as he was much alive on 2 April 1836 and located in St. Augustine. If he died in Paris as many contemporary writers said then he must have broken a record for rapid transit.

Bulow death records located

James Fiske a board member of the Flagler County Historical Society located a death and a burial record from Trinity Church in St. Augustine on microfilm at the St. Augustine history society library.

This record placed John Joachim Bulow's burial as May 8 1836, officiating clergy as a Rev. Davis. Place of burial was shown with 'ditto marks' on the report which were typical for the many Protestant burials in the Huguenot graveyard.

A notice also appeared in the Florida Herald Newspaper on May 11. 1836:

Notice: six weeks after date I will apply to the Hon. the Judge of the County Court of St. Johns County for letters of administration in the estate of J.J. Bulow Dec. – James K Anderson.

Also on 21 May 1836 a death notice appeared in the Charleston Observer saying that J .J. Bulow had died in St. Augustine on **Saturday night 7 May 1836**. This most likely was placed by his uncle.

The Militia soldiers in St. Augustine certainly would be in a bad frame of mind toward someone they believed was friendly toward the Indians.

Here are my own thoughts about John Joachim Bulow

and how he may have died that Saturday.

1. **He was sent to France as a young boy** educated there and almost certainly had "Parisian manners" which would not make him popular with the rustic Mosquito Roarers. Emily was 'born' on March 20 1804 after Charles Wilhelm Bulow married Adelaide Fowler Johnston on 16 January 1803. We do not know why her younger brother (born in 1807) was sent to Paris for his education in 1812.

2. **He was known to enjoy** good wines and drink.

3. **He did not agree with the 'Indian Removal'** and fired a small cannon at them (probably with powder only) as soldiers entered his grounds. He was furious at the occupation of his plantation and made his views very clear. He was arrested, locked up, and finally sent back with the refugees and wounded soldiers without being able to take any of his funds, articles or personal effects to St. Augustine.

4. **He was not popular** with the other planters. English visitor John Bemrose who was present in St. Augustine wrote the unflattering account saying Bulow was "Dissipated, and quarrelsome with his equals, tyrannical to his dependents..." which was strong stuff indicating Bemrose for sure did not care for him. Yet Bulow had a very successful plantation. Some of the other planters were deep in debt with heavy mortgages, perhaps causing some jealousy. "a quarrelsome nature" might be a hint.

5. **Times were wild when Bulow died.** He most likely would have been buried with only a wooden grave marker soon to be lost. If he were shot, or killed by an angry Militiaman then burial would be a quick one without formality.

Would he have killed himself? This does not seem to be in line with his character. Gen. Hernandez and others later made efforts to re-build or re-activate their plantations after the war. Bulow certainly still had the resources to do this. His plantation was very successful and showed his ability to manage perhaps with help of manager Francesco Pellicer. There is no indication he had a bad relationship with Mr. Pellicer.

SEARCH FOR THE LOST PLANTATIONS OF FLAGLER COUNTY

Was May of 1836 a sick season in St. Augustine? St. John's death records kept by the St. Augustine history library show no unusual sickness deaths around May 1836. [153] Their microfilm shows the death John J. Bulow but gives no detail as did other records of deaths. He was an important man but we found no written accounts of his death except for the notices already mentioned here.

The resting place and the manner of his death for John Joachim Bulow is not known. I have made several attempts to interest Florida archeological groups who may have ground penetrating radar. Perhaps there would be a skeleton with a bullet hole lying next to his father?

The Huguenot Cemetery is normally not open to casual visitors. I was drawn there to photograph the site on a Memorial Day when American flags were being placed on graves in the Huguenot Cemetery and entry was permitted. I had a strong feeling as I saw the flickering bright sun patterns filtered through the trees at the spot of the father Charles Wilhelm's burial.

"Here I lie" was the message I received as my camera recorded the spot.

25th CONGRESS, [SENATE.] [36]
2nd Session.

DOCUMENTS
IN RELATION
TO THE CLAIM OF THE EXECUTOR OF JOHN J. BULOW, Jr.,

To be indemnified for the loss of property destroyed by the hostile Seminole Indians.

To the honorable the Senate and House of Representatives of the United States of America in Congress assembled:

This petition respectfully showeth: That John J. Bulow, jr., has been a sufferer to a great extent by the wars in Florida; that his house, his crops, &c., have been burnt and destroyed by the Seminole Indians. That his house was occupied as a military post, picketed and garrisoned. Your petitioner has understood that, whatever may be the result of the general application of the citizens of Florida to be paid for their losses, Congress has never refused to pay for property destroyed by the enemy, if the property so destroyed was occupied by the troops or the militia of the United States as a military position. To prove the fact that it was so occupied, and to ascertain the amount of damage, your petitioner begs to refer to the accompanying certificates of the major and the general in command, and to the affidavits of respectable gentlemen whose names are thereto attached. He understands that the justice of claims like this has often been admitted, and the principle and precedent acknowledged and established, in the case of the inhabitants of the Niagara frontier, during the late war with Great Britain. He therefore prays Congress to take the case into consideration, and pass a law for the settlement of the claim.

W. G. BUCKNOR, *Executor.*

The claim of William Bucknor (Husband of Emily Bulow) in January of 1846 before Congress was not successful although all involved stated that the Bulow Plantation was destroyed because it had been occupied by the army and was thus entitled under law to be recompensed. Gen. Hernandez also made claim for over $100,000 for his losses, and after much effort in Washington a award was given of $34,521 about 1/3 of his claim in 1842. [154]

47 - Florida's Atlantic Side Plantations

Land grants, purchases of lands and many inheritances make up the enterprises that existed in Florida prior to the disaster of the 1835 Seminole War. Besides the major sites, there were many smaller holdings that are forgotten. After the British departed their large grants were divided into smaller sections as new Spanish land grants were offered. Sales and mergers happened yielding a multitude of active plantations south of Flagler, most of them located along Florida's Atlantic coast. Here are just a few of them:

Ormond (Damietta) part of James Moncrief grant of British period (1763 – 1784) Obtained by Capt. James Ormond in 1807. Located at head of Halifax River. James Ormond II took over when Capt. Ormond was murdered by run-away slave. In 1829 James Ormond III briefly ran plantation. Today it is located in Ormond Beach off the Old Dixie Highway between Tomoka and Bulow Plantation Ruins State Parks and is site of James Ormond II grave.

McHardy Robert McHardy was given a Spanish grant in 1815. It was part of the old and abandoned British John Moultrie Plantation. Like Mr. Clarke, McHardy was a surveyor for the Spanish Government. The property was purchased by the Marquis Des Fougiers and took the Rosetta name of the old Moultrie Plantation. It was once described as being one of the most valuable in Florida with over 500 acres of rich hammock land in cultivation. During Seminole War it was the first destination of Major Putnam and his "Mosquito Roarer" militia who arrived there on 21 December 1835. Putnam's group then had to retreat to the Bulow Plantation seven days later.

Dummett John Bunch was given a Spanish grant in 1804. It was originally part of John Moultrie's Rosetta Plantation. The lands were used by Bunch for 20 years. Sold to Capt. Thomas H. Dummett, a British Marine officer, in 1825. He installed equipment to operate one of the first steam powered sugar mills in Florida. Later owned by James K. Anderson. Part of Bulow Creek State Park. On Old Dixie

Highway two miles north of Tomoka State Park entrance.

Mount Oswald part of British grant of 20,000 acres to Richard Oswald in 1766. Operated by an agent. Sometimes called "The Ferry Tract" from ferry barge on Tomoka River. Mount Oswald is a major part of the Tomoka State Park. Abandoned and divided into separate plantations after the British departure.

Addison's Plantation Spanish grant of 1816. Part of Addison's Dummett property was purchased by Kenneth and Duncan McRae in 1825, also putting in a steam powered mill and utilizing Addison buildings. Location also called Carrickfergus. Ruins now identified as State Historic Sites.

Yonge Plantation originally part of 1764 Richard Oswald British grant. In 1803 Henry Yonge given Spanish grant near present Ormond Beach. Called Three Chimney location it is listed as Florida Historical site.

Orange Grove Plantation (near present Daytona Beach) Spanish grant to Samuel Williams for loyalty to Spanish government during the rebellion. 3,200 acres 10 miles north of Mosquito (now Ponce Inlet). Samuel died in 1813, his widow Ana had petitioned for control, but married Joseph Hernandez and thus secured her claim in 1817. A son, William Williams was with the Mosquito Roarer Militia group and had an angry argument with young Bulow as the rough army group was riding to Rosetta.

Dunlawton Plantation Part of the British Turnbull grant. In 1804 Patrick Dean obtained a Spanish grant. He was killed by an Indian and his nephew John Bunch obtained the property. In 1832 it was sold to the Anderson family of Sarah, George and James. The location is adjacent to Port Orange. The Anderson brothers operated this sugar plantation and mill until it was attacked and destroyed by Indians in 1835. The mill was rebuilt in the 1840's and operated up to the Civil War period. Ruins are preserved in a park called Sugar Mill gardens. Here was the battle between the Seminoles and the Florida Militia who had travelled by boat from the Bulow plantation in January of 1836.

Turnbull's New Smyrna Colony

SEARCH FOR THE LOST PLANTATIONS OF FLAGLER COUNTY

What could possibly go wrong?
Some 86 years ago historian and author Wilbur Henry Siebert wrote **Loyalists in East Florida 1774 to 1785**. Many books and accounts have been written about the Florida Minorcans and the failed colony. Here is his excellent writing:

DR. ANDREW TURNBULL and NEW SMYRNA COLONY [155]

After obtaining an order in council for 20,000 acres of land in East Florida in June, 1766, Dr. Turnbull sailed from England with his family and arrived at St. Augustine in the following November. He consulted the government surveyor as to where the best lands were to be found, visited Mosquito [now Ponce de Leon] Inlet, and there bought a large plantation, at the same time directing his overseer to purchase cattle from Georgia and Carolina. Returning to England by the last of March, 1767, he petitioned for permission to establish a colony and entered into an agreement with Sir William Duncan and Sir Richard Temple to that end, the latter being trustee for Lord George Grenville, head of the ministry, and his heirs. The partners obtained five large grants, in addition to Turnbull's, making a total of 101,400 acres. The lords of trade furnished a sloop-of-war for transportation, granted £4,500 as bounty on East Florida products to promote the settlement, and set apart sums for roads, bridges, ferries, and a parson and schoolmaster.

In the spring of 1767, Dr. Turnbull sailed to Greece and took on board two hundred mountaineers, thence to Leghorn and embarked one hundred and ten Italians, and so to Minorca for the rest of his settlers, numbering eleven hundred. Eight ships were required to carry the entire company to Florida, the expense being about £24,000, one-half being borne by Sir William Duncan and the other by Lord Grenville. Cotton gins, other agricultural machines, and the cuttings of olive and mulberry trees and grapevines were also brought. The passengers came as indented servants and, after paying for their passage and support by seven or eight years of labor, the adults were to receive fifty acres each and five acres for each child in a family. Four of the ships arrived at St. Augustine in June, 1768, and the others soon after. The colonists were sent down to Mosquito [now Ponce de Leon] Inlet, a part by land and a part by water. Five hundred Negroes were imported from Africa to clear the land and do other rough work, but were lost on the Florida coast. Up to July 21, 1769, the lords of the treasury paid £29,000 in support of the colony. In the following year an additional sum of £2,000 was entrusted to Governor Grant and expended for corn, which he distributed among the people of New Smyrna. The colony had been so named by Dr. Turnbull from Smyrna on the west coast of Asia Minor, the native place of his wife, who was a Greek. In 1772, indigo to the value of £3,300, the produce of a single year, was shipped to England from New Smyrna in exchange for articles exported to the settlement. By this time a tract of upwards of seven miles in length on the Halifax and Hillsborough rivers had been cleared, occupied, and cultivated, and more than a hundred houses had been built, including the town itself. Until 1779, Dr. Turnbull, as manager of the colony, expended its annual produce in its development, partly in remittances to England, South Carolina, Philadelphia, and New York for goods. He lived in a stone mansion four miles back from the settlement.

In May, 1767, Dr. Turnbull had been appointed a member of the provincial council, its clerk, and also secretary of the province by Governor James Grant. When the latter left East Florida in March, 1771, a number of the prominent inhabitants, including the officers of Fort George, desired that Turnbull be made his successor; but John Moultrie was appointed lieutenant governor, and failed to win the support of Turnbull and his friends, including Chief Justice William Drayton. Soon after Colonel Patrick Tonyn assumed the office of governor on March 1, 1774, he began to side with Lieutenant Governor Moultrie, and became even more distrustful of Drayton and Turnbull after finding that they were involved in a scheme to lease the Appalachee Old Fields from the Indians. After the outbreak of the Revolution, Governor Tonyn went so far as to declare that he did not believe that there were six loyal men in East Florida. This unwarranted statement was resented by Turnbull and his faction, who held a meeting in St. Augustine late in February, 1776, and adopted an address of loyalty to the king. Departing for England without procuring the permission of Tonyn, Turnbull and Drayton were suspended from their offices by the governor and council, but had the satisfaction of presenting their loyal address to Lord Germain and a few months later of submitting memorials to the lords of trade giving reasons for the removal of Tonyn. Later Turnbull answered the charges filed against him so satisfactorily that he was able to bring back, in the autumn of 1777, an order for his reinstatement.

During Turnbull's absence the colony at New Smyrna had been broken up. Disease had carried off about nine hundred of the settlers by 1773, malaria spread by swarms of mosquitoes being the chief cause. In 1776, the governor had drafted a company of militia from the colony, and his agents spread the story that the settlers, being Catholics, would not get title deeds to their lands since the terms of the grants specified Protestants. In May, 1777, some of the colonists appeared in St. Augustine, and preferred charges against their patron. The court of sessions imprisoned most of the plaintiffs and gave them only bread and water until they consented to fulfill their contracts at New Smyrna. Governor Tonyn, however, sent them other provisions by the hand of the sheriff and required Turnbull's attorneys to pay for the same. He also supported them in repudiating their contracts and gaining their release. They had made depositions containing serious charges against Dr. Turnbull, namely, that he had refused to release some of them when their time had expired, that he used a forged contract to prolong the service of an overseer, and that he had been guilty of certain violent crimes. Late in the summer of 1777, the rest of the colonists removed to St. Augustine, and a number soon took service in the militia or on board the provincial galleys. Several scores of them died during weeks of exposure in St. Augustine before small lots were set apart north of the town for the survivors to build their hovels on.

Dr. Turnbull returned from England in November, 1777, and in August, 1778, removed with his family from New Smyrna to St. Augustine. He now attempted to resume his offices, but the governor resisted and again suspended him in the latter part of 1778. Turnbull's partners were now dead, and their heirs, Lady Mary Duncan and the sons of Lord Grenville, brought suit for debt. Tonyn served as their attorney, hailed Turnbull before himself as judge in the court of chancery, involved him in an expense of more than four hundred guineas to defend himself, and lest he should leave East Florida required him to give bond in the sum of £4,000. Unable to do this, Turnbull came under the custody of the provost marshal and so remained for nearly two years. Meanwhile, he protested vigorously against the injustice of the whole procedure, and was released early in May, 1781, on condition of surrendering all but a small part of his share of New Smyrna. The property was now distributed among the other claimants.

As Dr. Turnbull feared further imprisonment, he left East Florida at once with his family in a small sloop and arrived at Charleston, South Carolina, on May 13, 1781. Another sloop containing what was left of his effects was captured. Tonyn endeavored to induce Lord Cornwallis and Brigadier General Alexander Leslie to expel Turnbull from Charleston, but without success. Dr. and Mrs. Turnbull spent the rest of their days there. James Penman had accompanied them on this voyage. A committee of the legislature gave the Turnbulls the privilege of remaining in the town after its evacuation, which took place in December, 1782. The doctor sent his resignation as secretary of East Florida to Lord Germain, and it was accepted. He entered upon the practice of his profession, and became one of the earliest members of the South Carolina Medical Society.

On May 22, 1786, Dr. Turnbull executed a power of attorney to Mr. Penman, then a merchant in London, to seek and receive compensation for the losses of himself and his four children, Nichol, Mary, Jean, and Margaret, due to the cession of East Florida to Spain. In the report of the commissioners for East Florida claims of March 14., 1788, the claims "examined and liquidated" include:

No. 122. Dr. Andrew Turnbull for £6462 10S real property. Awarded nothing.

No. 142. Dr. Andrew Turnbull for self and children, £15,057 10s. Awarded £916 13s* 4d (*about $4,500)

Dr. Turnbull died in Charleston on March 13, 1792. His Greek wife, Marcia Gracia Turnbull, who had been born in Smyrna, Asia Minor, after which the colony had been named, survived her husband until August 2, 1798, and was buried in St. Philip's churchyard at Charleston. *in 1927 currency

Cruger and Depeyster

Ambrose Hull was awarded a 1812 Spanish grant for two locations on the former British Turnbull New Smyrna grant near Mosquito Inlet. His executor sold the land in 1830 to William Depeyster and Henry N. Cruger who were from New York. Included were steam engines, many items, and slaves. The extensive sugar works was destroyed during the Seminole War and remains as a State of Florida Park. For many years local residents believed it was part of a Spanish Mission chain due to the artistic stone work of the ruins. This was disproven by Florida archeologists. The ruins of the Sugar Mill remain to exhibit the construction skill of the slave workers. Their dimensions were found to be very similar to those at the Bulow Sugar Mill ruins.

48 - The Early Plantations Are Gone

After 1840 when the U.S. army declared victory over the Seminoles (someone forgot to tell the Seminoles about this) and departed for the coming war with Mexico, the area that would become Flagler county was mostly a wilderness. Some smaller holdings remained, but the big plantations with machinery and numbers of slaves here did not exist. Timbering became the major enterprise. Live Oaks were in particular demand for ship building. Later would come naval stores including turpentine production which would later grow into a major industry even lasting up to the 1950's.

During the Civil War men made much needed salt along the ocean possibly using some salvaged sugar kettles from the now destroyed plantation works to boil away the sea water. Herds of cattle, perhaps some descendents of the Spanish cows were driven north on Old King's Road to feed the Confederate soldiers.

Narrow gauge railroads would arrive to reach small towns that grew across the county. By the 1900's modern

Florida started to appear when land developers offered thousands of prime acres for sale. The great plantations vanished. In their place grew such small communities as Favoreta, Relay, Neoga, Dupont, St. John's Park, Matanzas, Duke, Bimini, Dinner Island, Haw Creek, Orange Hammock, Cody's Corners, Espanola in 1894 and Bunnell. These and other towns then changed or vanished as modern highways replaced the old railroads where there is only a faint shadow of their presence. The great railroad connections of Dupont Center are replaced by auto junk yards south on U.S. highway 1. To replace the almost vanished 1774 Old King's Road (still in local usage right up to 1914) came the Dixie Highway of 1915 vintage intended to bring tourists from as far as Sault St. Marie Michigan to Miami Beach Florida. It twisted its way through what had become Flagler County. Today it's called 'the old brick road' but only a short 10 mile stretch still exists from Espanola to Hastings.

Finally the great city of Palm Coast arrived to cover much of what was once the great wetland of Graham's Swamp.

Memories of the great plantations that were once here have faded and exist mostly in scrapbooks and family Bibles with the "old families" many of whom still live in Flagler.

If you are fortunate to visit the town of Bunnell Florida on a Wednesday seek out historian Sisco Deen at the small green 'annex' building located behind the historic Holden House Museum. Here you might find old maps, photographs and some tales of our "Lost Plantations" in his collections.

History exists here in old Flagler County Florida.

It awaits your finding.

49 - Memories of the Past

Historian Sisco Deen is said to be related to almost all the "old families" in Flagler County. His collection of old documents, maps and records rest in a small green building that hides behind the 100-year-old Holden House Museum in the small town of Bunnell Florida. A few aging local historians meet here weekly to speak of times past.

Waves of history have washed against this community, often not for its best.

It would be wonderful to find some relics of the great colonial enterprises that were certainly here in this once totally agricultural county. Some still exist here as shown by the recently acknowledged site of "Hernandez" or "Long's Landing." There are still relics hiding in the Florida white sand. Early entrepreneurs such as Dupont, Bulow, Grisham, Hernandez should be remembered, or perhaps have a marker set in a Florida shopping mall to reflect that others were here too, now so long ago.

I followed Sisco Deen's old map, then the wonders of the internet, and finally some very old and rare books that showed other's research, the digitized Spanish land grants, and the British Colonial era written so well by William Henry Siebert back in the 1920's. The records of the violent Seminole War written in a huge volume by John T. Sprague, and all the other fading documents in the Deen collections are guides to our community memory that often drift away as Florida rapidly changes.

I do not know as much as I would desire concerning slaves in Flagler County. I found few first hand records and only hints of what was here.

Perhaps with this book some more stories will appear.

50 - I Became a Teller of Stories

I am a teller of stories. When I moved to Flagler County Florida so many years ago from "up north" I was fortunate to meet a group of wonderful historians such as Al Hadeed, the amazing collector of information Sisco Deen, Ed Moore at the Flagler Beach Museum and Robert Creal, plus Diane Marquis, Mary Ann Clark, re-enactors James Fiske and James Bullock and so many others. William Lenssen shared stories of the Bulow family. There were many others.

Sisco Deen collector of history

There are immense files of data, writings and photographs in the Flagler County Historical Society Annex, the Flagler Beach Museum, and the Clegg Collection at the Flagler County Public Library. One of the great collectors is Sisco Deen, descendent of one of the "early settler families."

Recently, a group of concerned Flagler citizens formed a Bulow Parks Alliance group to further support the remarkable history that exists in this Florida County. All too often our heritage falls beneath the bulldozer of the developer or can vanish beneath a shopping center, unknown and forgotten. We cherish the pieces that remain and those that try to protect and record them.

There are many lost stories in Flagler County. I can bring only a few together here, and much depends on those collectors of information who have been before me. It seems to be an endless task and I must begin somewhere. How about here?

Bill Ryan Palm Coast Florida – September 2015

About the Author

William P. Ryan (Bill) retired to Palm Coast Florida with his wife Pat after some 65 years in the high technology photographic industry. His technical interests and early experience as a journalist (Buffalo Evening News and Courier Express) later brought him some fame as a speaker and writer for groups such as The Professional Photographers of America, where he was awarded the degree of "craftsman," the White House Press Photographers, and other groups where he introduced new lighting techniques for color illustration. He was CEO of several well-known technical equipment marketing companies and guided the design of one of the first digital color print systems using high quality photo color paper.

Early in his career he worked in the Professional Products Advertising Department of Ansco, Binghamton, N.Y., one of America's oldest photo firms. Here he became involved in photo history via original plates and prints of Civil War Photographer Mathew Brady then at Ansco. His career and contacts took him too many European and Asian countries via the then international photographic industry.

Arriving in Florida in 1991 Bill helped to create Flagler County's first Internet site, back in its primitive days. This experience exposed him to the history of Flagler County located between St. Augustine and Daytona Beach on Florida's Atlantic Coast.

Bill Ryan loves to collect stories, often those never told or known before. He writes in a first person style and tells how many of these stories arrived at his door sometimes in an amazing manner. He is not a professional historian but writes what he believes "really did happen" based on his original documents and research.

Contact me:
I would like to hear from you,
Bill Ryan bpryan50@gmail.com

Endnotes

1 Ibid *Palm Coast Cultural Resources Assessment* pg 10 "Dupont Mill"

2 Interview with Mr. Hewitt J. Dupont

3 *Johnhorse.com* research website by Prof. J.B. Bird. The story of John Horse and the Black Seminoles, the first black rebels to beat American slavery and leaders of the largest slave rebellion in U.S. history—*an original history written & designed for the Web.*

4 *Palm Coast Cultural Resource Assessment* by Miller, James J., July 1978 with additional grants shown on Goold T. Butler, C.E. map Flagler County Florida 1926 *Flagler County Historical Society Archive*

5 *Floridamemories.com* / Spanish Land Grants in Florida

6 Ibid *Florida Memories*

7 Ibid Mr. Hewitt J. Dupont

8 *Clash between Cultures Spanish East Florida 1784-1821 El Escribino* by Jacqueline K. Fretwell and Susan R. Parker editors L David Norris pg 101-133

9 *Hernandez Holdings: Mala Compra and St. Joseph* by Harold D. Cardwell, Sr.

10 Collection *Territorial Papers of the United States* - Sisco Deen

11 *James Boswell* 1790, wonderful biographer and observer.

12 *Peter Buyck a Flemish American Revolutionary war financier* by John C. Hall, Otter Bay Books Baltimore Md. 2015

[13] Oct 10, 1823 Augustine Buyck and heirs of Josiah Dupont applied for ownership of a 30 acre island between the 'bars of Matanzas' inlet where their slaves made lime from shells (possibly Indian location) for many years citing grant to Josiah 9 August 1794. Application was refused.

[14] **Anne Goodbe Dupont** 1744-1805

[15] *Washington Oaks State Gardens Research Report* by Dr. Mildred L. Fryman Oct 1992 Colonial Periods pg 17

[16] **Clash Between Cultures** by Jane Landers *El Scribano* April 1988, Jorge Biassou, Black Chieftain.

[17] Original wedding document Dupont file, St. Augustine History Research Library.

[18] **Dupont papers** St. Augustine Historical Society reference library

[19] Compiled from translation Dupont Heir claims 1823, Floridamemories.com, **William Augustus Bowles** by Christopher Kimball in Southernhistory.us, files.usgwarchives.net/fl/stjohns/bios

[20] Ibid Dupont Heir claims dtd Oct 10, 1823 to U.S. Commission. **William Augustus Bowles** Alabama Heritage 103 winter 2012, University of Alabama by Susan Reynolds, mentions raid pg .26 "Indians plundered Dupong(sp), who lived about 30 miles south of Augustine of ten grown Negroes, and the same day killed a young man, named Bonnelly."

[21] Ibid *Florida Memories*

[22] 'Conflicts' *Washington Oaks State Gardens Research Report* by Dr. Mildred L. Fryman Oct 1992 pg 29 Hernandez family wrote Hernandez purchased MalaCompra from Michael Crosby in early 1816. **Palm Coast Cultural Resource Assessment** by Miller, James J., July 1978 page 113 wrote the grant purchased was that of the St. Joseph Plantation. (American State Papers, Vol IV:160) given as his reference. Research at

MalaCompra site and signage there indicated that MalaCompra was the lost Dupont original grant.

[23] Ibid ***Palm Coast Cultural Resource Assessment*** page 9 'Dupont house and cemetery'

[24] ***Palm Coast Cultural Resource Assessment*** by Miller James J. July 1978 page 151

[25] document Dupont folder, St. Augustine History library

[26] Reportedly buried in St. Augustine Huguenot Cemetery. Hewitt Dupont states this information is not correct. Abraham was wounded and died after the battle and is buried with 15,000 Confederate Soldiers in Oakwood Cemetery, Richmond, and William died April 5, 1862 in Volusia two months prior to date of the battle. Personal visit to grave site by Hewitt Dupont.

[27] ***Cornelius Dupont and family – the original settlers of Federal Point***, - federalpoint.tripod.com – by John R. Brown

[28] ***Palm Coast Cultural Resource Assessment*** by Miller James J. July 1978 pages 9-10

[29] ***Bulow estate claim documents*** Copies of the proceedings of a Court of Inquiry in relation to the Operations against the Seminole and Creek Indian" transmitted to the Honorable James K. Polk Speaker of the House of Representatives by the Secretary of War J. R. Poinsett on January 6, 1838. The proceedings were read, and laid upon the table on January 8, 1838 and published by the 25th Congress, 2nd Session as Document No. 78 January 20 1846 to U.S. Congress included in report #104 General Hernandez pg12, Sisco Deen collection.

[30] ***Memo Al Hadeed*** August 30 2013 "Historical Aspects of Linear Park and Longs Landing."

[31] Ibid Hadeed memo.

[32] Birth date research from Mildred L. Fryman PhD Oct 1992 as being 1792, others have birth date of 1793

[33] **Flagler Archaeological and Historic Sites** symposium report March 22, 2010 Art Dycke, Sisco Deen, Bill Ryan - City of Palm Coast

[34] Ibid **Flagler Archaeological and Historic Sites**

[35] Ibid *Hadeed* memo August 30, 2013

[36] *Washington Oaks State Gardens Research Report* by Dr. Mildred L. Fryman Oct 1992 pg 47

[37] *Palm Coast Cultural Resource Assessment* by Miller James J. July 1978

[38] *The Flagler Tribune* 10 May 1969 Sisco Deen Collection

[39] Ibid Washington State Gardens

[40] Original ltrs Flagler County Historical Society

[41] *The Spaniards in Florida comprising the notable settlement of the Huguenots in 1564* by George R. Fairbanks, President Florida Historical Society, Jacksonville FL 1868

[42] *A class of people neither freemen nor slaves* by Daniel L. Schafer University of Florida 1993 Journal of Social History Oxford University Press.

[43] *History of Volusia County Florida* by Pleasant Daniel Gold pg. 42 Painter Printing 1927

[44] **Abraham** was a much used interpreter. His eye was injured in the explosion of the "Negro Fort" during Jackson's 1816 invasion of Florida.

45 *WPA Spanish Land Grants.* Schene, Hopes, pg 30 Tallahassee 1941

46 'borrow pit' is a pond created by removal of earth for construction.

47 **Map East coast Florida** William G. deBraum, author's collection.
(This is only a partial list of names.)

48 **History of Volusia County Florida** by Pleasant Daniel Gold 1927 pg. 25

49 **Turnbull/Grant letters** author's collection from St. Augustine Historical Society Library.

50 Ibid **Palm Coast Cultural Resources Assessment** report

51 **Loyalists in East Florida 1774 to 1785** by Wilbur Henry Siebert Vol. II, page 74 Daytona Beach City Island Library.

52 **Ibid** page 76

53 **Ibid** page 81

54 material compiled from **Palm Coast Cultural Resources Assessment** by Miller, James J. July 1978 and **Letters of Dr. Andrew Turnbull** University of Florida, Florida History on Line

55 **Palm Coast Cultural Resource Assessment** by Miller James J. July 1978 page 115-116

56 **Ibid** page 80

57 **Ibid** pg 142-143

58 **flaglercountyfamilies.com** by Sisco Deen **Dupont**

[59] http://www.wikitree.com/wiki/Fish-1992

[60] Ibid

[61] *Palm Coast Cultural Resource Assessment* by Miller James J. July 1978 pages 10-151

[62] http://www.wikitree.com/wiki/Fish-1992

[63] *Dead Lake* was named for being the last stop for regular steam boat service to the St. John's Park area. Here is the Bull Creek fish camp which is presently a Flagler County park location.

[64] **Oliver presentation to U.S. Commission** August 31, 1825 *Florida Memories, Spanish Land Grants.*

[65] Ibid *Florida Memories* Spanish Land Grants Kingsley Dunn's Lake

[66] Ibid *Florida Memories* Santos Rodriguez

[67] *The King's Road Florida's first highway* by Dr. William R Adams, Daniel Schafer, Robert Steinbach, Paul Weaver – paper report 1997 - William Ryan collection.

[68] *Engineering Issues – American Society of Civil Engineers* June 1977 issue - William Ryan collection.

[69] *Ruins of the early plantations of the Halifax area* by Edith P. Stanton. 1949 Flagler County Historical Annex collection.

[70] *Ashes on the Wind* by Alice Strickland, Volusia County Historical

[71] Notes from Historic Properties survey by Sisco Deen

72 Ibid Strickland

73 **Clash Between Two Cultures East Florida 1784-1821** *El Escribino 1988* Thomas Graham St. Augustine Historical Society

74 **Yesterday's Reflections II** Nassau County Florida by Jan H. Johannes, Sr. January 2000

75 **East Florida as a refuge of southern loyalists, 1774-1785** by Wilbur H. Siebert 1927 American Antiquarian Society paper pg16

76 **A British Period Sawmill** by William M. Jones, original document report Aug 14 1978 – Sisco Deen Collection, Flagler County Historical Society

77 **The King's Road Florida's First Highway** – report Dr. William R. Adams 1977 Flagler County Historical Annex.

78 Ibid **A British Period Sawmill**

79 **Florida Master Site file** 8FL140 Flagler Ft. Fulton March 1988 Belle Terre Middle School. Buddy Taylor W. Ryan collection

80 Ibid **Palm Coast Cultural Resource Assessment** July 1978

81 Ibid **Resource Assessment**

82 **Spain's Two Florida's East and West** by Thomas Graham 'Clash between Cultures" St. Augustine Historical Society 1988

83 **John Russell family research paper** by Joyce Louise Russell Bevel dtd June 2004 Flagler County Historical Society archive

84 Ibid Russell paper

[85] ***The Bulow Plantation*** 1821-1835 by Ruth Danenhower Wilson – Florida Historical Quarterly April 1945

[86] ***Black Seminoles, Maroons & Freedom Seekers in Florida*** Africana Heritage Project

[87] **Bulow Estate Papers** John Rodman, 29 Nov. 1823 Florida Memories file

[88] ***palmettoroots.org/Family_Bulow*** by Carl W. Nichols author of *The Bulow family in South Carolina and Florida*

[89] ***The Bulow empire kingdom in the wilderness*** by Edward Stone, Sandlapper Magazine October 1973

[90] ***Yesterday's Reflections II*** Nassau County Florida by Jan H. Johannes, Sr. January 2000

[91] Ibid **Bulow Estate Papers**, John Rodman, 29 Nov. 1823

[92] **Charles W. Bulow will** microfilm St. Augustine historical association library.

[93] Ibid John Russell family research paper

[94] ***loridamemory.com***/Collections Bulow estate papers 29 Nov. 1823 St. Augustine

[95] ***Fifteen Years on Bulow Creek: Glimpses of Bulowville*** by Henry A. Baker The Florida Anthropologist March-June 1999

[96] ***Statement of losses sustained by John J. Bulow Jr.*** George L. Phillips Justice of the Peace 2 April 1836 Sisco Deen private collection

[97] ***Division order dtd 29 July 1867*** St. Johns County W Ryan collection trustees David R. Dunham, Virgil R. Dupont, Charles Lincoln

[98] *measuringworth.com* – modern value of money

[99] **Manuscript reminiscences of James Ormond III** Feb 3, 1892 pg 8 Flagler County Historical Society

[100] **Fifteen Years on Bulow Creek** by Henry Baker, University of Florida digital collection-June 1999

[101] **Out of the Land of Forgetfulness: Archaeological Investigations at Bulow Plantation** (8FL7) Flagler County Florida by Rebecca Claire O'sullivan January 2012

[102] **The first generation of Pellicers** by Donald F. Pellicer St. Augustine Historical Soc. Research Library

[103] **Bulow/Bucknor papers 1836-1896** Florida Historical Society visit and review by author

[104] **The Bulow Plantation 1821-1835** by Ruth Danenhower Wilson Florida Historical Quarterly Apr 1945

[105] **Sweet Cane The Architecture of the Sugar Work of East Florida** by Lucy B. Wayne pg 106 University of Alabama Press 2010

[106] **Florida Archaeological Reports** Griffin 1952, Daniel et al 1980 Baker No. 23 1982

[107] Ibid **Fifteen Years on Bulow Creek**

[108] **Journal of Social History,** Vol 26, No. 3 Spring, 1993, by Daniel L. Schafer, Oxford University Press

[109] Ibid **Reminiscences of James Ormond III**

[110] **Reminiscences of the Second Seminole War** by John Bemrose University of Florida Press 1966 edited John Mahon

[111] Ibid pg 12-13

[112] Ibid pg 12

[113] Ibid FloridaMemory.com Bulow estate papers

[114] Ibid *Sweet Cane*

[115] *Sweet Cane The Architecture of the Sugar Work of East Florida* by Lucy B. Wayne University of Alabama Press 2010

[116] floridahistoryonline/Plantations/plantations/Indigo_Cultivation_and_processing.htm

[117] Ibid *Fifteen Years on Bulow Creek* by Henry Baker

[118] unf.edu/floridahistoryonline/Plantations/plantations/Rice_Cultivation

[119] *The Birds of America* is a book by naturalist and painter John James Audubon, containing illustrations of a wide variety of birds of the United States. It was first published as a series in sections between 1827 and 1838, in Edinburgh and London.

[120] *A naturalist's excursion in Florida Audubon* ltr Dec 31, 1831, *Ashes on the Wind* by Alice Stickland

[121] "*Whaleboat*" Bulow's boat was referred to as a 'barge,' skiff', by others including Ormond III call it 'whale boat', races on the Halifax with a deep draft boat capable of being hoisted onto a ship. Also M.M. Cohen in 1836 *Notices of Florida*, and *Sketch of the Seminole War* by Dowling., both mention captured by Indians.

[122] *The Live Oakers* by Audubon Donald Held Rare books and maps audubongalleries.com – with permission.

[123] ***History of Flagler County*** John Clegg pg 23

[124] **Scipio** was a slave who vanished from the Bulow plantation when it was evacuated in January 1836. The name appears again in Florida history several times, and Mr. James Bullock reflected they may be related.

[125] Ibid ***Reminiscences of James Ormond III***

[126] Ibid ***The Bulow Plantation 1821-1835***

[127] Sprague, John T. ***The Origin, Progress and Conclusion of the Florida War,*** New York 1848 pg. 106

[128] ***George L. Phillips*** testimony Senate Claim Bucknor estate Sisco Deen collection

[129] Ibid George L. Phillips

[130] ***Bulow Claim June 1837 U.S. Congress*** – George L. Philips statements pg 13 – Sisco Deen Collection – Flagler County Historical Annex

[131] Ibid Philips

[132] ***John J. Bulow/Bucknor*** representative claims against US Congress Jan 20, 1846 Sisco Deen documents, claim of executor

[133] Letter Joseph Sanches Col. 2nd regiment to Mayor F. Weedon Dec 1835 – St. Augustine History Library

[134] ***Massacre!*** by Frank Laumer 1968 University of Florida Press

[135] ***Florida Historical Quarterly*** VIII pg. 188-196

[136] ***Testimony to U.S. Senate Hearing*** – C. Downing Feb 8 1839 Sisco Deen collection Flagler County Historical Society.

[137] Ibid Bulow/Bucknor estate claim Jan 20 1846

[138] **John S. Williams** testimony US Senate hearing Bucknor estate June 1837 Sisco Deen Collection

[139] Ibid testimony Benjamin Putnam

[140] ***Notices of Florida and the Campaigns*** by Cohen 1836 pg 96

[141] ***A sugar empire dissolves*** Florida Historical Quarterly 1951

[142] ***Ashes on the Wind*** by Alice Strickland pg 24 Volusia County Historical Commission

[143] ***The Dummett Family Saga*** by Alice Strickland pg 9, original print Florida Historical Society Quarterly.

[144] ***Washington Oaks State Gardens*** report by Mildred L. Fryman Ph.D. October 1992

[145] **Original news documents** Flagler County Historical Society

[146] ***Tustenuggee*** means Warrior or High Chief of War. He had hidden supplies at the Haw Creek location for many years.

[147] Sprague, John T. ***The Origin, Progress and Conclusion of the Florida War,*** New York 1848 pp 458, 481

[148] Ibid Sprague, John T. pp 398-400, 458, 481

[149] Ibid Sprague pg 481-482

[150] Ibid Sprague pg 486

[151] ***Inventory John Joachim Bulow estate*** 23 June 1841 fold3.com/image/#264148494

[152] ***The Bulow Empire Kingdom in the Wilderness*** by Edwin H. Stone, Sandlapper Magazine Oct 1973 (and others)

[153] Stauggens.com/stJohnsRecords/vitalRecords/DeathSJC1800s.html

[154] ***Washington Oaks State Gardens*** report by Mildred L. Fryman Ph.D. October 1992 page 44 Hernandez family.

[155] ***Loyalists in East Florida 1774 to 1785*** by Wilbur Henry Siebert, F.R.H.S. Research Professor in the Ohio State University, Volume II pg325 Florida State Historical Society 1929

Thank you to Sisco Deen for his image collection and records
Wikimedia Commons Pd-Art historical images
Floridamemories.com
Mary Ann Clark Flagler Historical Society
James Bullock Historical re-enactor St. Augustine
James Fiske President Bulow and Tomoka Park CSO
www.johnhorse.com Prof. J.B. Bird

Made in the USA
Columbia, SC
16 December 2018